PUBLISHER COMMENTARY

There is a reason the U.S. Air Force has one of the best cyberwarfare weapon system programs. This book pulls together 4 key Air Force publications on the Cyber Squadron Initiative (CS-I).

AFGM2017-17-01	CYBER SQUADRON INITIATIVE (CS-I)	11 Oct 2017
AFI 10-1703, VOL. 1	CYBERCREW TRAINING	2 Apr 2014
AFI 10-1703, VOL. 2	CYBERCREW STANDARDIZATION AND EVALUATION PROGRAM	15 Oct 2014
AFI 10-1703, VOL. 3	CYBERSPACE OPERATIONS AND PROCEDURES	6 May 2015

The Cyber Squadron Initiative (CS-I) is a transformational program to align Air Force communications units to evolving joint and service Cyberspace Operations doctrine, and to support major commands in effectively organizing, training and equipping the Cyberspace Operations Workforce. CS-I will refocus and strengthen traditional Air Force communications units in delivering enhanced mission assurance of wing-level assigned and attached weapons and mission systems to maintain operational advantage across the Air Force's five core missions.

AFI 10-1703 ensures all cybercrew members obtain and maintain the certification/qualification and proficiency needed to effectively perform their unit's mission. It applies to cybercrew positions that are designated mission ready/combat mission ready (MR/CMR). It establishes the Cybercrew Standardization and Evaluation (Stan/Eval) Program that supports Air Force objectives and provides guidance on how to structure and monitor a stan/eval program. It also establishes procedures for personnel assigned to Air Force cyber weapon systems.

If your organization is not following this guidance, then you are at a severe disadvantage. Air Force has been doing this for a while and they provide defensive and operational guidance that can be followed universally to protect critical computer networks.

Why buy a book you can download for free? We print this so you don't have to.

When a new standard is released, an engineer prints it out, punches holes and puts it in a 3-ring binder. While this is not a big deal for a 5 or 10-page document, many cyber documents are over 100 pages and printing a large document is a time-consuming effort. So, an engineer that's paid $75 an hour is spending hours simply printing out the tools needed to do the job. That's time that could be better spent doing engineering. We publish these documents so engineers can focus on what they were hired to do – engineering.

A list of **Cybersecurity Standards** we publish is attached at the end of this document.

Other titles published by 4th Watch Publishing Co.

DEPARTMENT OF THE AIR FORCE

WASHINGTON DC

MEMORANDUM FOR DISTRIBUTION C
MAJCOMs/FOAs/DRUs

FROM: SAF/CIO A6
1800 Air Force Pentagon
Washington DC 20330-1800

SUBJECT: Cyber Squadron Initiative (CS-I)

ACCESSIBILITY: Publication is available for downloading on the e-Publishing web site at
www.e-Publishing.af.mil.

RELEASABILITY: There are no releasability restrictions on this publication.

Compliance with this Memorandum is mandatory. To the extent its directions are inconsistent with other Air Force publications, the information herein prevails, in accordance with AFI 33-360, *Publications and Forms Management.*

By Order of the Secretary of the Air Force, this Air Force Guidance Memorandum immediately implements Cyber Squadron Initiatives. CS-I is a transformational program to align Air Force (AF) communications units to evolving joint and service Cyberspace Operations doctrine, and to support major commands (MAJCOM) in effectively organizing, training and equipping the Cyberspace Operations Workforce. CS-I will refocus and strengthen traditional AF communications units in delivering enhanced mission assurance of wing-level assigned and attached weapons and mission systems to maintain operational advantage across the Air Forces's five core missions. The CS-I is now transitioning from the Pathfinder program into an operationalization period for select AF units.

To begin the phased transition to CS-I, MAJCOMs, when requested by the SAF/CIO A6S, will provide a prioritized unit nomination list to receive approval to establish Mission Defense Teams (MDT) where relevant and feasible. From FY18 through FY24, SAF/CIO A6S will select 15 CS-I transition units per year based on MAJCOM input, mission need, and CS-I Pathfinder unit lessons learned. SAF/CIO A6S selected units will receive equipment and training for each MDT to protect a single priority mission or weapon system. MAJCOMs may opt to fund additional MDTs contingent upon sufficient training and equipment availability. Not all AF communication units will have a mission requirement to establish an MDT, but may transition other aspects of the CS-I in later stages depending on their enduring mission support requirements and available resources. There is potential for a unit outside of a traditional communication unit to receive authorization to stand up an MDT, on a case-by-case basis, without follow-on steps to fully transition to CS-I based on MAJCOM nomination.

CS-I Pathfinder units from FY16 and FY17 will continue to inform the MDT foundational concepts in an advisory role to their respective MAJCOMs, SAF/CIO A6S, as well as provide mentorship for new transitioning teams for a timeframe envisioned from FY18 - FY20 with pairing based on mission to maximum extent possible. CS-I Pathfinder and transitioning units are empowered to tailor processes to operationalize active defense capabilities to provide mission assurance and report those processes to their respective MAJCOMs and SAF/CIO A6S.

This Guidance Memorandum will serve as the bridge for the Pathfinder and transitioning units until the CS-I Program Action Directive is approved. Please use this initial guidance to empower coordination with other functional communities to accomplish initial essential actions.

Ensure that all records created due to processes prescribed in this publication are maintained in accordance with the Air Force Records Disposition Schedule (RDS) located in the Air Force Records Information Management System (AFRIMS).

This directive applies to all military and civilian Air Force personnel, the Air Force Reserve (AFR), and Air National Guard (ANG). This Memorandum becomes void after one year has elapsed from the date of this Memorandum, or upon release of a new Air Force publication permanently establishing this guidance, whichever is earlier.

PATRICK C. HIGBY, Maj Gen, USAF
Director, Cyberspace Strategy and Policy

Attachment: CS-I Roles and Responsibilities

Attachment

CYBER SQUADRON INITIATIVE (CS-I) ROLES AND RESPONSIBILITIES

1. Roles and Responsibilities. Roles and responsibilities for the Cyber Squadron Initiative (CS-I) are a coordinated effort between all organizations fielding, supporting, and utilizing Mission Defense Teams (MDT) AF functional communities will have primary or supporting roles.

1.1. Cyberspace Strategy and Policy Director (SAF/CIO A6S). SAF/CIO A6S, as the chair of the CS-I Steering Group, has overall responsibility for the CS-I. SAF/CIO A6S will:

1.1.1. Provide strategy, policy, guidance, and oversight for the CS-I, including leadership of established sub-working groups.

1.1.2. Select 15 MDT teams per year for HAF-funded transition to the CS-I. Also, approve any MAJCOM funded transition units for inclusinon into the CS-I transition.

1.1.3. Coordinate funding for initial MDT equipment purchase and specified initial training for HAF-funded CSI units.

1.1.4. Develop metrics to assess progress, develop lessons learned, and inform the future CS-I efforts.

1.2. Major Commands (MAJCOMs). MAJCOMs will:

1.2.1. Nominate units for transition to the CS-I or remove or reallocate existing unit MDTs as nessisary in coordination with the SAF/CIO A6S.

1.2.2. Ensure nominated units are prioritized and meet criteria set from SAF/CIO A6S.

1.2.3. Accept service delivery degradation risk for personnel reallocation to support CS-I or provide resourcing to mitigate the risk for selected units.

1.3. Selected Unit Commanders. Commanders will:

1.3.1. Assign personnel to stand up MDT and ensure assigned personnel use government-provided equipment for official authorized use only.

1.3.2. Track and report assigned metrics during the standup of MDTs, to include mandatory organizing, training, and equipping steps, and inform on other points of interest as required by SAF/CIO A6S related to the CS-I transition implementation.

1.3.3. Ensure coordination with protected mission owners, Program Management Offices, Assigned Intelligence Providers and other requisite functional communities to facilitate the identification of Key Terrain – Cyberspace as an outcome of the MDT-conducted Functional Mission Analysis.

1.3.4 Ensure the completion of MDT initial and follow-on skills training for all assigned members.

DEPARTMENT OF THE AIR FORCE
WASHINGTON, DC

AFI10-1703V1_AFGM2017-01

22 February 2017

MEMORANDUM FOR DISTRIBUTION C
MAJCOMs/FOAs/DRUs

FROM: SAF/CIO A6
1480 Air Force Pentagon
Washington, DC 20330-1480

SUBJECT: Air Force Guidance Memorandum to AFI 10-1703, Volume 1, *Cybercrew Training*

By Order of the Secretary of the Air Force, this Air Force Guidance Memorandum immediately changes Air Force Instruction 10-1703, Volume 1, *Cybercrew Training*, 2 April 2014. Compliance with this Memorandum is mandatory. To the extent its directions are inconsistent with other Air Force publications, the information herein prevails, in accordance with AFI 33-360, *Publications and Forms Management*. Ensure that all records created as a result of processes prescribed in this publication are maintained IAW Air Force Manual (AFMAN) 33-363, *Management of Records*, and disposed of IAW Air Force Records Information Management System (AFRIMS) Records Disposition Schedule (RDS).

As a result of the publication of AF Policy Directive 17-2, *Cyberspace Operations*, which supersedes AFPD 10-17, *Cyberspace Operations*, dated 31 July 2012; AFI 10-1703, Volume 1 is hereby renumbered as AFI 17-202, Volume 1. This Memorandum is a renumbering of AFI 10-1703 only; the title and content remain unchanged. I hereby direct the Office of Primary Responsibility (OPR) for AFI 10-1703 to conduct a special review in accordance with AFI 33-360 to align its content with AFPD 17-2. This will result in a rewrite or rescind action of AFI 10-1703.

This Memorandum becomes void after one year has elapsed from the date of this Memorandum, or upon incorporation by interim change to, or rewrite of AFI 10-1703, Volume 1, whichever is earlier.

WILLIAM J. BENDER, Lt Gen, USAF
Chief of Information Dominance and Chief
Information Officer

BY ORDER OF THE SECRETARY
OF THE AIR FORCE

AIR FORCE INSTRUCTION 10-1703,
VOLUME 1

2 APRIL 2014

Incorporating Change 1, 6 May 2015

Operations

CYBERCREW TRAINING

COMPLIANCE WITH THIS PUBLICATION IS MANDATORY

ACCESSIBILITY: Publications and forms are available on the e-Publishing website at www.e-Publishing.af.mil for downloading or ordering

RELEASABILITY: There are no releasability restrictions on this publication

OPR: AF/A6SS

Certified by: AF/A3C/A6C
(Maj Gen Earl D. Matthews)
Pages: 18

This instruction implements Air Force Policy Directive (AFPD) 10-17, *Cyberspace Operations*. This instruction establishes the Cybercrew Training Program (CTP) that supports Air Force (AF) objectives and provides guidance on how to structure and monitor a cyber training program. This publication applies to all military and civilian AF personnel, members of the AF Reserve Command (AFRC), Air National Guard (ANG), third-party governmental employee and contractor support personnel in accordance with appropriate provisions contained in memoranda support agreements and AF contracts. This instruction requires collecting and maintaining information protected by the Privacy Act of 1974 (*5 U.S.C. 552a*). System of Records Notices F036 AF PC C, Military Personnel Records System, and OPM/GOVT-1, *General Personnel Records*, apply. Units may supplement this instruction. Coordinate supplements through HQ AFSPC/A3T prior to publication. Coordinate MAJCOM supplements with AF/A6SS. Guidance provided by the lead major command should contain specific training requirements unique to individual and crew positions. Send recommended changes or comments to HQ USAF/A6SS, 1480 Air Force Pentagon, Washington, DC 20330-1480, through appropriate channels, using AF Form 847, *Recommendation for Change of Publication*. When collecting and maintaining information protect it by the Privacy Act of 1974 authorized by 10 U.S.C. 8013. Ensure that all records created as a result of processes prescribed in this publication are maintained in accordance with AFMAN 33-363, *Management of Records*, and disposed of in accordance with the AF Records Disposition Schedule (RDS) located in the AF Records Management Information System (AFRIMS). See attachment 1 for a glossary of references and supporting information.

SUMMARY OF CHANGES

This interim change revises AFI 10-1703, Volume 1, by incorporating changes identified during the compliance statement review and updating office symbols and references. Several tiering codes have been updated and related language changed to improve readability and clarify responsibilities.

1. General. This instruction prescribes basic policy and guidance for training AF cybercrews according to AFPD 10-17.

1.1. **Program Goals**. The AF CTP ensures all cybercrew members obtain and maintain the certification/qualification and proficiency needed to effectively perform their unit's mission. The objective of the CTP is to develop and maintain a high state of mission readiness for immediate and effective employment across the full range of military operations, while structuring each training mission to achieve optimum training experience.

1.1.1. Cybercrews consist of individuals who conduct cyberspace operations and are assigned to a specific cyber weapon system. Personnel who perform cyberspace intelligence, surveillance, and reconnaissance (ISR) functions do not fall under the purview of this instruction; training for these personnel is addressed in the 14-2XX series of AF Instructions.

1.1.2. This AFI applies to cybercrew positions that are designated mission ready/combat mission ready (MR/CMR) in guidance provided by the lead major command. Personnel filling MR/CMR positions at the 624 OC and the 960 CyOG-Det 1 (854th Command Control Squadron (CSS) (AFRC)) will adhere to guidance in Paragraphs 1 through 1.3.5.6, and applicable Lead MAJCOM provided policy and guidance.

1.1.3. Individuals who perform cyberspace support functions but are not assigned to a MR/CMR crew position within a weapon system follow the Quality Assurance policy in AFI 33-150, *Management of Cyberspace Support Activities*, and/or AFI 36-2201, *Air Force Training Program*, as applicable.

1.2. **Waiver Authority**. The authorities to waive wing/unit level requirements in this publication are identified with a Tier ("T-0, T-1, T-2, T-3") number following the compliance statement. See AFI 33-360, Publications and Forms Management, Table 1.1 for a description of the authorities associated with the Tier numbers. Submit requests for waivers as described in this paragraph.

1.2.1. HQ USAF/A6SS is the waiver authority for this instruction. Unless otherwise noted, HQ USAF/A6SS delegates waiver authority to HQ AFSPC/A3T. Waiver authority may not be further delegated.

1.2.2. Forward all waiver requests via email through the applicable Group/CC, NAF/A3 or NAF/OV (as applicable), to HQ AFSPC/A3T. Describe the specific requirement, state the reason a waiver is required, and include proposed risk management steps, as needed. Specify an expiration date for the waiver, if applicable. Intermediate command levels should recommend approval or disapproval of the waiver request.

1.2.3. If approved, waivers remain in effect for the life of the published guidance, unless HQ AFSPC/A3T specifies a shorter period of time, cancels in writing, or issues a change that alters the basis for the waiver.

1.2.4. AF Reserve Units. HQ AFRC/A3T is the waiver authority for this instruction for reserve units. AFSPC gained units process waivers IAW paragraph 1.2. The reserve group commander submits waiver requests through 10 AF/A3 to HQ AFRC/A3T. HQ AFRC/A3T provides a copy of the waiver request and HQ AFRC/A3T waiver decision to HQ AFSPC/A3T.

1.3. **Responsibilities**.

1.3.1. HQ USAF/A3C/A6C:

1.3.1.1. Formulates cybercrew training Concept of Operations (CONOPS).

1.3.1.2. Sets policy and guidance for the conduct and execution of the cybercrew training program, in coordination with the Lead MAJCOM.

1.3.1.3. Oversees development and management of cybercrew weapon system designations.

1.3.1.4. Oversees Lead MAJCOM development and management of all cyber policy and guidance documents.

1.3.1.5. Monitors and reviews MAJCOM programs to ensure MAJCOM policies, guidance and instruction supplements are adequate.

1.3.1.6. Hosts training conferences annually, or as required, to assist in maintaining appropriate commonality and identify shortfalls in cybercrew training programs. Base the attendee list on conference topics.

1.3.1.7. Coordinates cyber intelligence, surveillance and reconnaissance (ISR) requirements with HQ USAF/A2D.

1.3.2. HQ USAF/A2:

1.3.2.1. Formulates cyberspace ISR training requirements and manages ISR-related training issues.

1.3.2.2. Coordinates cyberspace ISR training requirements and issues with HQ USAF/A3C/A6C and HQ AFSPC/A3T as required.

1.3.3. HQ AFSPC (As Lead MAJCOM):

1.3.3.1. Develops and manages cybercrew weapon system designations.

1.3.3.2. Develops and manages, in coordination with user commands, the appropriate guidance documents to establish cybercrew training requirements and standards, regardless of mission designation and command of assignment. Refer to Attachment 2 for information on training development.

1.3.3.3. Hosts annual, or as required, weapon system-specific training conferences to review all programs for currency, applicability, compliance, and effectiveness, and address issues in lead command-provided guidance documents as appropriate. Attendees should include training representatives from career field managers, user commands, formal schools, Numbered Air Force (NAF) training and stan/eval offices (if applicable), and selected unit representatives. Submit formal training requirements to career field managers for incorporation in Utilization & Training Workshop process as defined in AFI 36-2201.

1.3.3.4. Determines total force cybercrew training requirements in coordination with National Guard Bureau (NGB)/AF Reserve Command (AFRC) across the FYDP. Forward requirements annually to HQ USAF/A3C/A6C, via the Program Requirements Document (PRD), for validation and inclusion in the Undergraduate and Graduate PGLs.

1.3.3.5. Follows AFPD 10-9, *Lead Command Designation and Responsibilities for Weapon Systems*, for additional responsibilities.

1.3.4. All MAJCOMs (with assigned cybercrews IAW para 1.1 and AFPD 10-17).

1.3.4.1. Establish a cybercrew training office responsible for the overall management of the command's cybercrew training program. (Air National Guard (ANG) is considered a MAJCOM for purposes of this instruction.)

1.3.4.2. Maintain oversight of cybercrew training within its chain of command and for attached units and gained units.

1.3.4.3. Convene conferences and working groups, as necessary, to review and improve training policies and procedures.

1.3.4.4. Send proposals for amending existing formal school course prerequisites and syllabi or deleting obsolete courses to the training command for approval.

1.3.5. All NAFs (with assigned cybercrews IAW para 1.1).

1.3.5.1. Establish a cybercrew training office responsible for the overall management of the cybercrew training program.

1.3.5.2. Maintain oversight of cybercrew training within its chain of command and for attached units and gained units.

1.3.5.3. Convene conferences and working groups, as necessary, to review and improve training policies and procedures.

1.3.6. Training Command.

1.3.6.1. Is a command which operates a cyber weapon system and provides operational training for cybercrews.

1.3.6.2. Maintains quota allocation and management responsibilities.

1.3.6.3. Captures inputs from Air Staff, AFPC, lead and user MAJCOMs, and other users in the allocation of training quotas in order to fulfill maximum total force training requirements within programmed capacity.

1.3.6.4. Approves formal school courses and syllabi in coordination with lead commands and program managers.

1.3.6.5. Develops, updates, and maintains courseware and training syllabi to support Mission Essential Tasks (METs). Performs task and media analysis associated with cybercrew qualification training per AFI 36-2201; AFI 36-2251, *Management of Air Force Training Systems*; and function as the approving authority for these courses (coordinates with the lead command if different than the training command).

1.3.6.6. Outlines procedures for a Progress Review (PR) to be accomplished when a student fails to progress according to syllabus requirements.

2. Qualification Training. This section defines cybercrew operational status and specifies minimum training requirements for Initial Qualification Training (IQT) and Mission Qualification Training (MQT).

2.1. **Cybercrew Operational Status.** A cybercrew member may be assigned Basic Cyber Qualified (BCQ), Basic Mission Capable (BMC), or Mission Ready/Combat Mission Ready (MR/CMR) status.

2.1.1. Basic Cyber Qualified (BCQ). A cybercrew member who has satisfactorily completed IQT.

2.1.2. Basic Mission Capable (BMC). A cybercrew member who has satisfactorily completed IQT and MQT, but is not in fully-certified MR/CMR status. The cybercrew member must be able to attain MR/CMR status to meet operational taskings as specified in the applicable lead MAJCOM-provided guidance **(T-1)**. Identify BMC requirements in the applicable lead MAJCOM-provided guidance.

2.1.3. Mission Ready (MR)/Combat Mission Ready (CMR). A cybercrew member who has satisfactorily completed IQT and MQT, and maintains certification, currency and proficiency in the command or unit operational mission is MR. A cybercrew member who has satisfactorily completed IQT and MQT, and maintains certification, currency and proficiency in the command or unit combat mission is CMR. Minimum requirements include:

2.1.3.1. Completion of IQT, MQT, and a formal Stan/Eval evaluation.

2.1.3.2. Certifying Official's (first operational commander in the member's chain of command, or his/her designee) certification as well as certification of completion of unit-designated crew force management requirements.

2.1.3.3. Once a certifying official (or his/her designee) certifies an individual as MR/CMR, the individual maintains MR/CMR status based on Continuation Training (CT) requirements identified in paragraph 3.

2.2. Initial Qualification Training (IQT). One or more courses covering system specific and/or positional specific training as a prerequisite to Mission Qualification Training (MQT).

2.2.1. Method. Unless otherwise specified in applicable lead MAJCOM guidance, the primary method of IQT is to attend and complete the appropriate formal training course(s) listed in the Education and Training Course Announcement (ETCA) found at **https://etca.randolph.af.mil**, USAF Formal Schools. Completing the appropriate formal course(s) satisfies all IQT requirements.

2.2.2. In-Unit IQT. When formal course attendance is not practical or quotas are not available, units will request waivers to conduct in-unit IQT, using formal school courseware, as specified in the applicable lead MAJCOM- provided guidance **(T-2)**. Accomplish in-unit training IAW applicable formal school courseware and the following guidance: **(T-2)**:

2.2.2.1. Training lessons should be completed in order; however, if mission scheduling or student progress dictates otherwise, the unit commander or designee may change the order.

2.2.2.2. Training syllabi establish a maximum time period between training events. Failure to accomplish training as scheduled requires documentation and corrective action.

2.2.2.3. With operations group commander (OG/CC) (or equivalent) approval, IQT requirements may be completed during operational missions under the supervision of an instructor certified on the task of like specialty. Comply with restrictions in appropriate lead MAJCOM-provided guidance, MAJCOM directives, and applicable operation orders (OPORD).

2.2.2.4. Cybercrew members participating in in-unit IQT are dedicated to that training, which takes priority over non-training related duties. *EXCEPTION:* Supervisory personnel may continue their normal duties as time permits.

2.2.3. IQT Prerequisites. The Cyber Unit's Training OIC must ensure each cybercrew member complies with the appropriate formal course training prerequisites prescribed in the applicable syllabus, before entering qualification training **(T-2)**.

2.3. Mission Qualification Training (MQT). MQT prepares an individual for a successful formal evaluation. It focuses on filling training requirements not met at IQT, mastering local procedures, and increasing proficiency as needed. MQT ensures a smooth transition from IQT to MR/CMR status.

2.3.1. Method. MQT is comprised of training at a Formal Training Unit (FTU), if applicable, and local training at the unit. Units determine MQT requirements IAW lead MAJCOM policy and guidance. Cybercrew members participating in in-unit MQT are dedicated to that training, which takes priority over non-training related duties. *EXCEPTION:* Supervisory personnel may continue their normal duties as time permits.

2.3.2. MQT Prerequisites. Each cybercrew member must complete all applicable IQT requirements IAW para 2.2 before entering MQT **(T-2)**.

2.3.3. Time Limits. Training time limitations for MQT completion are contained in applicable lead MAJCOM-provided guidance. The AF member will begin In-unit MQT no later than 45 days (90 days for the Active Reserve Component) after reporting to a new duty station or unit, unless waived by the MAJCOM cybercrew training function **(T-2)**.

2.4. **Requalification Training.** A cybercrew member is considered unqualified upon loss of currency exceeding 6 months, expiration of his or her qualification evaluation, or completion of a qualification evaluation in a different weapon system (unless multiple qualification has been approved prior to the evaluation), whichever occurs first. The duration of unqualified time is measured from the date the cybercrew member became unqualified until the specific retraining start date. An unqualified cybercrew member can requalify IAW the following:

2.4.1. Loss of currency 6-12 months: Completion of training in all delinquent items (as applicable), additional training as directed by the certifying official and a requalification evaluation IAW AFI 10-1703 Volume 2.

2.4.2. Loss of currency exceeding 12 months: Recompletion of MQT and a requalification evaluation IAW AFI 10-1703 Volume 2.

2.4.3. Expiration of qualification evaluation not exceeding 6 months: Completion of training in all delinquent items (as applicable), additional training as directed by the certifying official, and a requalification evaluation AFI 10-1703 Volume 2.

2.4.4. Expiration of qualification evaluation exceeding 6 months: Recompletion of MQT and a requalification evaluation IAW AFI 10-1703 Volume 2.

3. Continuation Training (CT). Training that provides crew members with the volume, frequency, and mix of training necessary to maintain proficiency in the assigned position and at the designated certification/qualification level. This training is identified within the respective lead MAJCOM-provided guidance.

3.1. **Currency.** Currency requirements for cybercrew members are identified within the respective lead MAJCOM-provided guidance.

3.2. **Recurrency Training.** A cybercrew member is considered not current upon loss of currency as specified in the applicable lead MAJCOM-provided guidance. If currency is lost for up to six months, the cybercrew member must demonstrate proficiency with an instructor in all delinquent items **(T-2)**.

3.3. **Responsibilities.**

3.3.1. Squadron Commander. The squadron commander or designated representative will ensure individuals receive training to successfully attain/maintain required certifications/qualifications, complete unit missions and maintain individual proficiency **(T-2)**.

3.3.2. Cybercrew Members. Each cybercrew member is responsible for monitoring and completing all training requirements.

3.4. Failure to Complete Continuation Training Requirements.

3.4.1. Report individuals in Status of Resources and Training System (SORTS) IAW AFI 10-201, *Status of Resources and Training System (SORTS)*, and/or IAW lead MAJCOM-provided guidance.

3.4.2. The training supervisors must ensure Individuals who fail to accomplish minimum CT requirements and subsequently lose currency are in a supervised status as specified in lead MAJCOM-provided guidance **(T-2)**.

3.4.3. The training supervisor will document decisions to suspend, retain, or downgrade a cybercrew member's status if the individual fails to meet the standards established by this AFI, AFI 10-1703, Volume 2, or lead MAJCOM-provided guidance, citing all which apply **(T-2)**.

4. Upgrade Training. Training needed to qualify to a cybercrew position of additional responsibility for a specific weapon system (e.g., from a crew member to a crew commander). See applicable lead MAJCOM-provided guidance for applicable positions, instructions, and additional requirements.

5. Multiple Qualification.

5.1. MAJCOMs may authorize qualification in more than one weapon system for crewmembers only when such action is directed by command mission requirements and is economically justifiable. This authority cannot be delegated below the MAJCOM level, except for the Lead MAJCOM, which may further delegate within its command, but not lower than wing commander.

5.2. Restriction on multiple qualification in para 5.1 does not apply to cybercrew members selected for reassignment to another weapon system who attend training prior to PCS.

6. Instructor Training and Certification. Instructors will complete appropriate training program and certification requirements, as specified in the appropriate lead MAJCOM-provided guidance **(T-2)**. Instructor trainees will be observed and supervised by the Chief of Training (or equivalent or their designee) **(T-2)**. Instructors will be current and certified in any task they instruct **(T-2)**. Supervisors will ensure that Instructor training consists of, at a minimum:

6.1. Applicable equipment configuration and scheduling procedures (e.g., simulator and on-line equipment configuration, instruction scenario control procedures) **(T-2)**.

6.2. Instructional System Development (ISD) process and procedures **(T-2)**.

6.3. Construction, conduct, and administration of classroom training as appropriate for the weapon system **(T-2)**.

6.4. Construction, conduct, and administration of simulator, ops floor, and field training as appropriate for the weapon system **(T-2)**.

6.5. Observance, at a minimum, of one certified instructor conducting training in the classroom, in the simulator, on the ops floor, and in the field, as appropriate for the weapon system **(T-2)**.

7. Cybercrews Operating on Non-US Air Force Weapon Systems and/or with Non-US Air Force Units. Air Force cybercrews performing appropriate duties on non-US Air Force systems, or on duty with or attached to non-US Air Force units for cyber operations, are only required to maintain their training records.

8. Documentation.

8.1. Cybercrew member training events are documented on the Air Force Form 4419, *Record of Training* **(T-2)**. Software applications capturing the same information are authorized provided they comply with lead MAJCOM-provided policy and guidance **(T-2)**.

8.2. Cybercrew member CT and additional training events are maintained in an Individual Qualification Folder (IQF). Electronic format IQFs are authorized provided proper security measures, backup capability, and sustainment plans are in place.

8.3. Dispose of IQFs and other related material according to the AF Records Disposition Schedule (RDS), and AF guidance concerning the protection of Personally Identifiable Information.

BURTON M. FIELD, Lt Gen, USAF
DCS Operations, Plans & Requirements

Attachment 1

GLOSSARY OF REFERENCES AND SUPPORTING INFORMATION

References

AFDD 3-12, *Cyber Operations*, 15 July 2010, with change 1, 30 November 2011

AF Doctrine Annex 3-12, Cyberspace Operations, 15 July 2010, with change 1, 30 November 2011

AFPD 10-17, *Cyberspace Operations*, 31 July 2012

AFPD 10-9, Lead Command Designation and Responsibilities for Weapon Systems, 8 May 2007

AFI 10-201, *Status of Resources and Training System (SORTS)*, 13 April 2006

AFI 10-201, Status of Resources and Training System (SORTS), 19 April 2013

AFI 14-2, *Intelligence Rules and Procedures*, 29 November 2007

AFI 33-150, *Management of Cyberspace Support Activities,* 30 November 2011.

AFI 36-2201, *Air Force Training Program*, 15 September 2010

AFI 36-2235, Volume 1, *Information for Designers of Instructional Systems - ISD Executive Summary for Commanders and Managers*, 2 September 2002

AFMAN 33-363, *Management of Records*, 1 March 2008

AFMAN 36-2234, Instructional Systems Development, 1 November 1993

Privacy Act of 1974 (5 United States Code [U.S.C.] 552a)

Privacy Act of 1974 (5 United States Code [U.S.C.] 552a)

Prescribed Forms

AF Form 4419, *Record of Training*.

Adopted Forms

AF Form 847, *Recommendation for Change of Publication*

Abbreviations and Acronyms

AFSC—Air Force Specialty Code

ANG—Air National Guard

ARC—Air Reserve Component (AFRC and ANG)

BCQ—Basic Cyber Qualified

BMC—Basic Mission Capable

CMR—Combat Mission Ready

CONOPS—Concept of Operations

CT—Continuation Training

CTP—Cybercrew Training Program

ETCA—Education and Training Course Announcement

FCR—Formal Course Review

FTU—Formal Training Unit

FYDP—Future Years Defense Program

IQF—Individual Qualification Folder

IQT—Initial Qualification Training

ISR—Intelligence, Surveillance, and Reconnaissance

MAJCOM—Major Command

MET—Mission Essential Tasks

MQT—Mission Qualification Training

MR—Mission Ready

NAF—Numbered Air Force

PGL—Program Guidance Letter

PR—Progress Review

PRD—Program Requirements Document

SORTS—Status of Resources and Training System

Terms

(UPDATED) Instructional System Development (ISD)— Instructional system development is a deliberate and orderly, but flexible process for planning, developing, implementing, and managing instructional systems. It ensures that personnel are taught in a cost-efficient way the knowledge, skills, and attitudes essential for successful job performance. (AFMAN 36-2234)

Basic Cyber Qualified— A cybercrew member who has satisfactorily completed IQT.

Basic Mission Capable— A cybercrew member who has satisfactorily completed IQT and MQT, but is not in fully-certified MR/CMR status. The cybercrew member must be able to attain MR/CMR status to meet operational taskings as specified in the applicable instructional supplements. This status is primarily for individuals in units that perform weapon system-specific operational support functions (i.e., formal training units, operational test and tactics development). BMC requirements will be identified in the appropriate lead MAJCOM-provided guidance.

Certification— Designation of an individual by the certifying official (or his/her designee) as having completed required training and evaluation and being capable of performing a specific duty.

Combat Mission Ready— A cybercrew member who has satisfactorily completed IQT and MQT, and maintains certification, currency and proficiency in the command or unit combat mission.

Continuation Training— Training which provides crew members with the volume, frequency, and mix of training necessary to maintain currency and proficiency in the assigned qualification level.

Currency— A measure of how frequently and/or recently a task is completed. Currency requirements should ensure the average cybercrew member maintains a minimum level of proficiency in a given event.

Cybercrew Members— Cybercrew members consist of individuals who conduct cyberspace operations or computer network exploitation and are typically assigned to a specific weapon system.

Cyber (adj.)— Of or pertaining to the cyberspace environment, capabilities, plans, or operations.

Cyberspace— A global domain within the information environment consisting of the interdependent network of information technology infrastructures and resident data, including the Internet, telecommunications networks, computer systems, and embedded processors and controllers. (JP 1-02)

Cyberspace Operations— The employment of cyberspace capabilities where the primary purpose is to achieve objectives in or through cyberspace. (Joint Pub 3-12)

Cyberspace Support— Foundational, continuous or responsive operations in order to ensure information integrity and availability in, through, or from Air Force-controlled infrastructure and its interconnected analog and digital portion of the battlespace. (AFPD 10-17)

Initial Qualification Training (IQT)— One or more courses covering system specific and/or positional specific training as a prerequisite to Mission Qualification Training (MQT).

Instructional System Development (ISD)— A systematic, flexible, proven process for determining whether instruction is necessary in a given situation, for defining what instruction is needed, and for ensuring development of effective, cost-efficient instruction. (AFI 36-2235, Volume 1)

Instructor— An experienced individual qualified to instruct other individuals in mission area academics and positional duties. Instructors will be qualified appropriately to the level of the training they provide.

Mission Ready— A cybercrew member who has satisfactorily completed IQT and MQT, and maintains certification, currency and proficiency in the command or unit operational mission.

Mission Qualification Training (MQT)— Training needed to qualify for cybercrew duties in an assigned crew position for a specific weapon system.

Requalification Training— Academic and positional training required to requalify to MR/CMR status.

Time Periods— The following definitions are provided for interpretation of timing requirements specified in this instruction:

Day— Unless otherwise specified, "day" means calendar days. When "work days" are specified, count only duty days. Do not count scheduled unit "down" days against this time limit.

Month— The term "month" means calendar months, not 30-day periods.

Unqualified— Previously CMR crewmembers whose CMR status has lapsed due to any of the reasons contained in paragraph 2.4.

Attachment 2

TRAINING DEVELOPMENT

A2.1. Training development: Will define the special set of skills required for mission accomplishment **(T-2)**. Applicable published training standards establish the minimum training task performance standards required and provide constraints for all performance scenarios. These will include all tasks/subtasks, along with associated performance standards, conditions, proficiency codes and applicable timing requirements **(T-2)**. For standardization levels see AFI 10-1703v2, *Cyberspace Operations Standardization and Evaluation (Stan/Eval) Program.*

A2.1.1. Tasks Standard Level Descriptions. Three task standard levels will be used for each task: A, B, and C **(T-2)**. All tasks/subtasks will be documented in a comprehensive task/sub-task list developed by the units, approved by the NAF, and coordinated through Lead MAJCOM/A3T **(T-2)**.

A2.1.2. Level A/Critical task/sub-task. Critical tasks are tasks that could result in mission failure, endangerment of human life, serious injury or death. Critical tasks have the greatest potential for extreme mission or personnel impacts and drive the most stringent training and evaluation program requirements. Critical tasks apply to time-sensitive tasks or tasks that must be accomplished as expeditiously as possible without any intervening lower priority actions that would, in the normal sequence of events, adversely affect task performance/outcome.

A2.1.3. Level B/Essential task/sub-task. Essential tasks are tasks deemed integral to the performance of other tasks and required to sustain acceptable weapon system operations and mission execution. Essential tasks drive significant training requirements.

A2.1.4. Level C/Non-Essential task/sub-task. Non-Essential tasks are rudimentary or simple tasks related to weapons system operations that by themselves have little or no impact on mission execution. Non-Essential tasks require the least stringent training requirements.

A2.1.5. Ensure the requirements contain detailed givens/constraints, performance, and standards for all critical tasks/subtasks (T-2).

A2.2. Use the sample Task/Subtask List: and task requirements tables on the next pages as examples only.

A2.3. Table A. 2.1 is an example only. CCC is cyber crew commander, CA is Cyber Analyst, and CO is Cyber Operator.

Table A2.1. (Sample) Task/Subtask List

AREA & TASK SUB-TASK	DESCRIPTION	33NWS						92IOS		
		Level	CCC	COC	CO	CA	COT	Level	CCC	CA
	MISSION SUPPORT OPERATIONS									
A01	**Perform Crew Actions**									
A01A	Perform Crew Changeover/Shift Actions	C	3c	3c	3b	1b	1b			
A01B	Perform Status of Manning Actions	B	3c	3c						
A01C	Log Operational Activities	B	3c	3c	3c	3c	3c			
A02	**Pre Mission Activities**									
A02A	Perform Tasking Coordination Activities							B	3c	
A02B	Perform Personnel Assignment Activities							B	3c	
A02C	Perform Equipment Preparation Activities							B	3c	3c
A02D	Perform Site Survey Activities							B	3c	3c
A02E	Perform Assessment Plan Activities							B	3c	3c
A02F	Perform Team Pre-Mission Activities							B	3c	3c
A03	**Post Mission Activities**									
A03A	Perform Reporting Activities							B	3c	3c
A03B	Perform Data Archival Activities							B	3c	3c
A03C	Perform Hot Wash Activities							B	3c	3c
A03D	Perform Equipment Return Activities							B	3c	3c
	STATUS MONITORING									
B01	**Perform Fault/Anomaly Resolution Procedures**									
B01A	Perform Mission System Outage Procedures	A	**3c**	**3c**	3c	3c	3c			
B01B	Perform Facility System Outage Procedures	A	3c	3c	3c	3c	3c			

AREA & TASK SUB-TASK	DESCRIPTION	33NWS Level	CCC	COC	CO	CA	COT	92IOS Level	CCC	CA
B01C	Perform Sensor Outage Reporting	B					3c			
B02	**Monitor Communication Channels**									
B02A	Manage Internal Communication	B	3c	3c	2c	1b	3c			
B02B	Manage External Communication	B	3c	3c	2c	1b	3c			
	MISSION PROCEDURES									
C01	**Perform INFOCON Procedures**	B	3c	3c						
C02	**Perform In-Brief Activities**							B	3c	
C03	**Perform Equipment Setup Activities**							B	2b	3c
C04	**Perform Collection Activities**							B	2b	3c
C05	**Perform Analysis and Validation Activities**							B	2b	3c
C06	**Perform Daily Reporting Activities**							B	3c	3c
C07	**Perform Non-Technical Assessment Activities**							B	2b	3c
C08	**Perform Equipment Breakdown Activities**							B	2b	3c
C09	**Perform Out-Brief Activities**							B	3c	
C10	**Perform Platform Operations (PO)**									
C10A	Perform ArcSight Console Operations	B	2c	2c	3c	3c				
C10B	Perform Sensor Operations	B	2c	2c	3c	3c				
C10C	Apply Sensor Signature Update	B					3c			
C11	**Perform Analyst Operations**									
C11A	Perform Channel Monitoring	A	1c	1c	3c	3c				
C11B	Perform Basic Event Analysis	A	1c	1c	3c	3c				

AREA & TASK / *SUB-TASK*	DESCRIPTION	33NWS						92IOS		
		Level	CCC	COC	CO	CA	COT	Level	CCC	CA
C11C	Perform Packet Retrieval	A	1c	1c	3c	3c				
C11D	Perform Packet Analysis	A	1c	1c	3c	3c				
C11E	Perform IP Blocking	B	2d	2d	3c	3c				
C11F	Perform Event Categorization	B	3d	3d	3c	3c				
C11G	Coordinate / Deconflict External Assessments	B	3c	3c	3c	2c				
C11H	Perform Advanced WireShark Operation	B	1c	1c	3c	3c				
C12	**Apply Network Security Principles (NS)**									
C12A	Identify Network Protocols	C	2c	2c	3c	3c				
C12B	Identify Network Security Threats	C	2c	2c	3c	3c				
C12C	Resolution Tools	C	2c	2c	3c	3c				
C13	**Execute Contingency Operations**									
C13A	Execute Continuity of Operations Plan (COOP)	B	3d	3d	3c	3c	3c			
C13B	Transition to Alternate Operating Location (AOL)	A	3d	3d	3c	3c	3c			
C14	**Utilize Reporting Tools / Procedures**									
C14A	Open and Edit ArcSight Cases	B	2c	2c	3c	3c				
C14B	Annotate Events	B	2c	2c	3c	3c				
C14C	Operate historical information database	B	3c	3c	3c	3c				
C14D	Event Investigation Handling	A	3c	3c	3c					
C14E	Incident Handling	A	3c	3c	3c					
C14F	Coordinate TCNO/C4NOTAM	B	3c	3c			3c			
C14G	Coordinate OPREP 3 Information Requirements	B	3c	3c				B		3c
C14H	Coordinate Reporting Products	B	3c	3c						
C14I	Conduct Online Collaborative Sessions	B	3c	3c						

AREA & TASK / SUB-TASK	DESCRIPTION	33NWS						92IOS		
		Level	CCC	COC	CO	CA	COT	Level	CCC	CA
	EMERGENCY PROCEDURES									
E01	Perform Emergency/Safety/Security/ Contingency Procedures									
E01A	Perform Fire Procedures	A	3c	3c	3c	3c	3c	C	3c	3c
E01B	Perform Bomb Threat Procedures	A	3c	3c	3c	3c	3c	C	3c	3c
E01C	Perform Accident/Injury/Illness Procedures	A	3c	3c	3c	3c	3c	C	3c	3c
E01D	Perform Severe Weather/Natural Disaster Procedures	A	3c	3c	3c	3c	3c	C	3c	3c
E01E	Perform Total Evacuation Procedures	A	3c	3c	3c	3c	3c	C	3c	3c
E01F	Perform Missing Crewmember Procedures	B	3c	3c	3c	3c	3c			

DEPARTMENT OF THE AIR FORCE
WASHINGTON, DC

AFI10-1703V2_AFGM2017-01

23 February 2017

MEMORANDUM FOR DISTRIBUTION C
                MAJCOMs/FOAs/DRUs

FROM: SAF/CIO A6
          1480 Air Force Pentagon
          Washington, DC 20330-1480

SUBJECT: Air Force Guidance Memorandum to AFI 10-1703, Volume 2, *Cybercrew Standardization and Evaluation Program*

By Order of the Secretary of the Air Force, this Air Force Guidance Memorandum immediately changes Air Force Instruction 10-1703, Volume 2, *Cybercrew Standardization and Evaluation Program*, 15 October 2014. Compliance with this Memorandum is mandatory. To the extent its directions are inconsistent with other Air Force publications, the information herein prevails, in accordance with AFI 33-360, *Publications and Forms Management*. Ensure that all records created as a result of processes prescribed in this publication are maintained IAW Air Force Manual (AFMAN) 33-363, *Management of Records*, and disposed of IAW Air Force Records Information Management System (AFRIMS) Records Disposition Schedule (RDS).

As a result of the publication of AF Policy Directive 17-2, *Cyberspace Operations*, which supersedes AFPD 10-17, *Cyberspace Operations*, dated 31 July 2012; AFI 10-1703, Volume 2 is hereby renumbered as AFI 17-202, Volume 2. This Memorandum is a renumbering of AFI 10-1703 only; the title and content remain unchanged. I hereby direct the Office of Primary Responsibility (OPR) for AFI 10-1703 to conduct a special review in accordance with AFI 33-360 to align its content with AFPD 17-2. This will result in a rewrite or rescind action of AFI 10-1703.

This Memorandum becomes void after one year has elapsed from the date of this Memorandum, or upon incorporation by interim change to, or rewrite of AFI 10-1703, Volume 2, whichever is earlier.

WILLIAM J. BENDER, Lt Gen, USAF
Chief of Information Dominance and Chief
Information Officer

BY ORDER OF THE SECRETARY
OF THE AIR FORCE

AIR FORCE INSTRUCTION 10-1703,
VOLUME 2

15 OCTOBER 2014

Incorporating Change 1, 2 JULY 2015

Operations

**CYBERCREW STANDARDIZATION
AND EVALUATION PROGRAM**

COMPLIANCE WITH THIS PUBLICATION IS MANDATORY

ACCESSIBILITY: Publications and forms are available on the e-Publishing website at
www.e-Publishing.af.mil for downloading or ordering

RELEASABILITY: There are no releasability restrictions on this publication

OPR: HQ USAF/A6SS

Certified by: HQ USAF/A6S
(Brig Gen Zabel)
Pages: 42

This instruction implements Air Force (AF) Policy Directive (AFPD) 10-17, *Cyberspace Operations*. It establishes the Cybercrew Standardization and Evaluation (Stan/Eval) Program that supports AF objectives and provides guidance on how to structure and monitor a stan/eval program. This publication applies to all military and civilian AF personnel, members of AF Reserve Command (AFRC) units and the Air National Guard (ANG). This publication may be supplemented at the unit level; route all direct supplements through channels to HQ USAF/A6S for coordination prior to certification and approval. Refer to lead MAJCOM-provided instructions for specific stan/eval requirements unique to individual and cybercrew positions. The authorities to waive wing/unit level requirements in this publication are identified with a Tier ("T-0, T-1, T-3, T-3") number following the compliance statement. See AFI 33-360, Publications and Forms Management, Table 1.1 for a description of the authorities associated with the Tier numbers. Send recommended changes or comments to the Office of Primary Responsibility (HQ USAF/A6SS, 1480 Air Force Pentagon, Washington, DC 20330-1480), using AF Form 847, *Recommendation for Change of Publication*; route AF Forms 847 from the field through the appropriate functional's chain of command. This instruction requires collecting and maintaining information protected by the Privacy Act of 1974 (*5 U.S.C. 552a*). System of records notices F036 AF PC C, Military Personnel Records System, and OPM/GOVT-1, *General Personnel Records*, apply. When collecting and maintaining information protect it by the Privacy Act of 1974 authorized by 10 U.S.C. 8013. Ensure that all records created as a result of processes prescribed in this publication are maintained in accordance with AFMAN 33-363, *Management of Records*, and disposed of in accordance with the AF Records Disposition Schedule (RDS) located in the AF Records Management Information System (AFRIMS). See Attachment 1 for a glossary of references and supporting information.

SUMMARY OF CHANGES

This interim change revises AFI 10-1703, Volume 2, by incorporating changes identified during the compliance statement review, and updating office symbols and references. Several tiering codes have been updated and related language changed to improve readability and clarify responsibilities.

Chapter 1

PURPOSE

1.1. General. The Cybercrew Stan/Eval Program provides commanders a tool to validate mission readiness and the effectiveness of unit cyberspace operations, including documentation of individual cybercrew member qualifications and capabilities.

1.1.1. Cybercrews consist of individuals who conduct cyberspace operations and are assigned to a specific cyberspace weapon system (CWS).

1.1.2. This Instruction applies to cybercrew positions that are designated mission ready (MR)/combat mission ready (CMR) in the applicable lead MAJCOM-provided guidance. Personnel filling MR/CMR positions at the 624 OC will adhere to guidance in Paragraphs 1.1 through 1.3.5, and applicable lead MAJCOM-provided guidance only. (T-2)

1.1.3. Individuals who perform cyberspace support functions and are not assigned a MR/CMR cybercrew position within a CWS follow the guidance for AF cyberspace support activities contained in AFI 33-150, *Management of Communications Activities*, and/or AFI 36-2201, *Air Force Training Program*, as applicable. Examples include, but are not limited to, Information Assurance professionals, network administrators, help desk personnel, and Communications Focal Point (CFP) technicians.

1.2. Objectives.

1.2.1. Provide a system to assess and document individual proficiency and capability to accomplish assigned cyberspace operations duties.

1.2.2. Develop and ensure standardization of operational procedures for CWS employment.

1.2.3. Ensure compliance with appropriate operational, training, and administrative directives.

1.2.4. Evaluate and revise operational directives, procedures, and techniques as necessary.

1.2.5. Recognize trends in order to recommend/initiate changes to training programs and directives.

1.3. Waiver Authority. Submit requests for waivers according to the instructions in this paragraph.

1.3.1. HQ AFSPC/A3T is the waiver authority for this instruction. Unless otherwise noted, waiver authority may be delegated to the appropriate Wing Commander, but may not be further delegated.

1.3.2. General Guidance. Provisions of this AFI may be waived by Wing, Group, or NAF Commanders with appropriate justification. Forward copies of all waivers granted to the next higher headquarters, and to HQ AFSPC/A3T and HQ AF/A6SS. AF Reserve and National Guard units will forward copies of waivers to HQ AFRC/A3T or NGB/A3, as appropriate, and to HQ AFSPC/A3T and HQ AF/A6SS. (T-1)

1.3.3. AF Reserve Units. Waiver authority granted in this instruction applies only to MR/CMR designation and does not extend to the waiver of AFSC-awarding requirements.

1.3.4. Air National Guard (ANG) units. NGB/A3C is the waiver authority for this instruction for ANG units. AFSPC gained units will process waivers IAW paragraph 1.3 through their appropriate ANG group commander where applicable. (T-2) The group/unit commander will submit waiver requests to NGB/A3C. (T-2) NGB/A3C will provide a copy of the waiver request and waiver decision to HQ AFSPC/A3T.

1.3.5. Waivers remain in effect for the life of the published guidance, unless a shorter period of time has been specified, the waiver is cancelled in writing, or a change to this AFI alters the basis for the waiver.

Chapter 2

HIGHER HEADQUARTERS (HHQ) STAN/EVAL FUNCTIONS AND ORGANIZATION

2.1. Scope. For the purposes of this instruction, HHQ includes Headquarters U.S. Air Force (HAF), MAJCOM, and NAF stan/eval functions.

2.2. Air Staff.

2.2.1. AF/A6S.

2.2.1.1. Sets policy and guides the conduct and execution of the Stan/Eval Program.

2.2.1.2. Assigns AF/A6SS as the Office of Primary Responsibility (OPR) for this Instruction.

2.2.1.3. Oversees development and management of all CWS policy documents.

2.2.2. AF/A6SS.

2.2.2.1. Reviews and maintains this instruction.

2.2.2.2. Reviews MAJCOM supplements to this AFI to ensure compliance with basic policy guidance in this instruction, as applicable.

2.2.2.3. Maintains liaison with HAF organizations, MAJCOMs, and cyber career field functional managers to ensure compliance by all cybercrew personnel.

2.2.2.4. Coordinates with HAF organizations and MAJCOM stan/eval functions to ensure lead MAJCOM-developed guidance conforms to and complies with basic AF policy guidance contained in this Instruction.

2.2.2.5. Oversees development and management of all lead MAJCOM-developed guidance documents.

2.3. MAJCOMs. The following guidance applies only to MAJCOMs designated as the lead command or as a using command for a CWS.

2.3.1. General.

2.3.1.1. MAJCOM stan/eval staffs are primarily responsible for establishing administrative processes. Lower echelons of command are primarily responsible for the cyberspace operations and evaluation functions.

2.3.1.2. MAJCOM stan/eval staffs may obtain MR/CMR certification in a cybercrew position to maintain functional expertise.

2.3.1.3. HAF, direct reporting units, and the ANG are considered MAJCOMs for the purpose of this instruction.

2.3.2. Functions.

2.3.2.1. The lead MAJCOM for each CWS will develop and manage applicable guidance.

2.3.2.1.1. MAJCOM functionals will determine CWS-specific operational guidance. Guidance provided by the lead MAJCOM will be no less restrictive than that contained in this AFI.

2.3.2.2. Convene conferences and working groups, as necessary, to review and improve command stan/eval policies and procedures.

2.3.2.3. Provide staff coordination and control of all Cybercrew Information File (CIF) items issued from the MAJCOM level to units (see Chapter 9).

2.3.2.4. Establish guidance for MAJCOM-mandated stan/eval software, when applicable.

2.3.2.5. Assist with the review, updating and distribution of CWS-specific Master Question Files (MQFs) as needed (see Chapter 7).

2.3.2.6. Coordinate on evaluation criteria and guidance in conjunction with the lead MAJCOM and other user MAJCOMs operating like CWSs.

2.3.2.7. Coordinate on and process applicable AF Forms 847 through stan/eval channels (Ops Group Stan/Eval (OGV), NAF (if applicable), and MAJCOM. ANG units will utilize the NAF/MAJCOM command structure with oversight responsibility. (T-2)

2.3.2.8. Review subordinate unit Stan/Eval Board (SEB) minutes and address any action items requiring HHQ assistance.

2.3.2.9. In the absence of a NAF stan/eval function, assume responsibilities listed in paragraph 2.4.

2.3.3. Organization.

2.3.3.1. MAJCOM Commanders will assign the MAJCOM/A3 (or equivalent) responsibility for the MAJCOM stan/eval program.

2.3.4. Augmentation. Each MAJCOM may use augmentees from other MAJCOMs to support or conduct cross-command stan/eval program reviews and evaluations with concurrence of all the MAJCOM stan/eval organizations involved. Augmentees will use the criteria of the MAJCOM they are augmenting. (T-2)

2.4. NAFs.

2.4.1. General. NAF stan/eval will maintain a tactical focus and perform the operational role in evaluating unit stan/eval functions within its chain of command. (T-2) MAJCOM stan/eval assumes these responsibilities when no NAF stan/eval exists.

2.4.2. Functions.

2.4.2.1. Provide oversight and guidance for stan/eval functions in lower echelon units, in gained units, and in aligned AFRC/ANG units.

2.4.2.2. Coordinate on and process applicable AF Forms 847 through stan/eval. ANG units will utilize the NAF/MAJCOM command structure with oversight responsibility. (T-2)

2.4.2.3. Provide staff coordination and control of all CIF items issued from the NAF level to units (see Chapter 8).

2.4.2.4. Provide qualified cyber examiners to augment other MAJCOM and NAF agencies when requested (see paragraph 2.3.4).

2.4.2.5. Administer objectivity evaluations, when practical, to chiefs of stan/eval or senior stan/eval crews in lower echelon units, in gained units, and in AFRC/ANG units for which oversight responsibility is assigned. NAF stan/eval personnel do not require cybercrew examiner certification to conduct objectivity evaluations.

2.4.2.6. Observe execution of unit missions and provide feedback when feasible.

2.4.2.7. Review subordinate unit SEB minutes and, at a minimum, address any action items requiring HHQ assistance.

2.4.2.8. Review and approve MQFs.

2.4.2.9. Review and approve evaluation criteria.

2.4.2.10. Review and coordinate on applicable lead MAJCOM-provided guidance.

2.4.3. Organization.

2.4.3.1. NAF commanders will designate the NAF/A3 (or equivalent) responsible for the NAF stan/eval program.

2.4.3.2. NAF stan/eval staff should be selected from personnel with cybercrew stan/eval experience when practical.

2.4.4. Augmentation. Each NAF may use qualified augmentees to support or conduct reviews, evaluations, and inspections with concurrence of all the NAF stan/eval organizations involved.

Chapter 3

UNIT STAN/EVAL FUNCTIONS AND ORGANIZATION

3.1. Scope. For purpose of this instruction, "unit" includes levels of organization under HHQ required to establish a stan/eval function. Most units are composed of an Operations Group (OG) and cyber squadrons/detachments (henceforth in this AFI, "Operations Group" will be considered any Group-level command, and "squadron" should be used synonymously with "detachment"). Where there is no parent OG, squadrons will assume duties listed for OGs. (T-2)

3.2. Operations Group Commander (OG/CC). When circumstances prohibit the OG/CC from executing these responsibilities, the MAJCOM/A3 may grant a written waiver allowing a squadron/detachment commander (Sq/Det/CC) to assume them. The OG/CC will:

3.2.1. Direct the conduct of the unit level stan/eval program **(T-3)**.

3.2.2. Provide manpower to the unit stan/eval function to execute the duties directed by this AFI **(T-3)**.

3.2.3. Designate OGV stan/eval examiners (SEE) (see section 4.2) **(T-3)**.

3.2.4. Designate additional cybercrew examiners who are not assigned to OGV, when necessary, to meet unique unit requirements. Document in the SEB minutes (see Attachment 4) **(T-3)**.

3.2.5. Designate, when necessary, stan/eval liaison officers (SELOs) to assist OGV in administrative duties **(T-3)**.

3.2.6. Chair the SEB **(T-3)**.

3.2.7. Establish procedures to implement MAJCOM-mandated stan/eval software, as necessary **(T-3)**.

3.2.8. Provide waiver authority for weapon system cybercrew examiners to evaluate mission/skill sets in which they are not certified **(T-3)**.

3.3. Stan/Eval Organization. The stan/eval function is normally administered from the group level (OGV) with the Chief of Stan/Eval reporting directly to the OG/CC. However, when circumstances prohibit, or if directed by the OG/CC, the Squadron/Detachment may assume responsibility for this function. Reserve this transfer of responsibility for units not collocated with the Group. The stan/eval function will:

3.3.1. Consist of a Chief of Stan/Eval and at least one examiner per cybercrew position per CWS. (T-3)

3.3.1.1. The OG/CC may determine if a specific examiner is not required based on unit requirements or personnel constraints. This should be indicated in the SEB minutes.

3.3.1.2. The Chief of Stan/Eval will be a certified examiner in a unit CWS **(T-3)** and report directly to, and be rated by, the OG/CC (or Sq/Det/CC when the function resides below group) **(T-3)**.

3.3.1.3. Commanders will ensure that examiners are selected from the most suitable, highest qualified and most experienced personnel **(T-3)**.

3.3.2. Process AF Form 4418, *Certificate of Cybercrew/Spacecrew Qualification* and AF Form 4420, *Individual's Record of Duties and Qualifications* **(T-3)**.

3.3.3. Establish, monitor, and maintain the unit Individual Qualification Folders (IQF) program IAW Chapter 8 **(T-3)**.

3.3.4. Establish procedures for review and quality control of evaluation documentation **(T-3)**.

3.3.5. Establish and maintain a trend analysis program IAW Chapter 9 **(T-3)**.

3.3.6. Conduct SEBs IAW Chapter 9 and ensure SEB minutes are distributed within 15 calendar days **(T-3)**. OG/CC determines the distribution, which at a minimum includes the NAF stan/eval function. **(T-3)**

3.3.7. Establish unit no-notice program and goals. **(T-3)** The stan/eval function will monitor this program to ensure goals set by the OG/CC or SQ/CC are met and unit no-notice evaluations are distributed proportionately among positions and types of evaluations **(T-3)**.

3.3.8. Design evaluation criteria and submit to NAF for review and approval IAW Attachment 3 **(T-3)**. Evaluation criteria require NAF approval prior to implementation.

3.3.9. Design Master Question Files (MQFs) for all CWSs assigned to the group and submit to NAF for review and approval IAW Attachment 2 **(T-3)**. MQFs require NAF approval prior to implementation.

3.3.10. Develop and document the SEE training program **(T-3)**, designed to instruct and certify SEEs on the proper manner in which to correctly assess cybercrew proficiency as part of their role in the Instructional Systems Development (ISD) process. Prior to implementation of the SEE training program, the appropriate NAF stan/eval will review and approve the program and ensure it meets the requirements of Chapter 4 **(T-3)**.

3.3.11. Monitor the upgrade and objectivity of all SEEs **(T-3)**.

3.3.12. At least quarterly, advise unit leadership on unit cybercrew qualification status, requisite completion, and upcoming expiration dates **(T-3)**. In addition, at least semi-annually the stan/eval function will advise unit leadership on unit trends as well as combined trends across all units under the stan/eval office's responsibility. **(T-3)**

3.4. Squadron Commander. Supports the group stan/eval program and encourages a positive climate conducive to successful implementation of the Cybercrew Standardization and Evaluation Program.

Chapter 4

CYBERCREW EXAMINERS

4.1. General. The evaluation portion of the Cybercrew Stan/Eval Program is administered by SEEs at both the group and squadron levels. An examiner who is qualified on more than one CWS may evaluate more than one position.

4.2. SEEs will:

4.2.1. Complete appropriate training program documented on AF Form 4420 before certification **(T-3)**. A certified SEE conducting the SEE training on another individual does not need to be appointed as an instructor. A certified SEE will observe and supervise evaluator trainees **(T-3)**. At a minimum the training consists of:

4.2.1.1. Applicable equipment configuration and scheduling procedures (e.g., simulator and on-line equipment configuration, test and evaluation scenario control procedures).

4.2.1.2. ISD process and procedures.

4.2.1.3. Construction, conduct, and administration of the written phase of an evaluation.

4.2.1.4. Construction, conduct, and administration of the performance phase of an evaluation.

4.2.1.5. Observance, at a minimum, of one certified SEE conducting an evaluation.

4.2.2. Conduct cybercrew evaluations IAW with this instruction. **(T-3)**

4.2.3. Maintain MR/CMR status in each position that they will evaluate **(T-3)**. NAF-level examiners are only required to maintain basic mission capable (BMC) status per the requirements in AFI 10-1703, Volume 1, *Cybercrew Training*.

4.2.4. Administer evaluations only in those positions in which they maintain qualification and certification. **(T-3)** Exception: spot qualification (SPOT) evaluations and where specifically authorized in applicable MAJCOM guidance.

4.2.5. Not administer evaluations outside of their MAJCOM unless specifically requested by the MAJCOM stan/eval organization of the examinee and approved by the MAJCOM stan/eval organization of the examiner **(T-2)**. MAJCOMs may establish procedures in their supplement for CWS cybercrew examiners to administer evaluations outside of NAFs/units within their own MAJCOM (see also paragraph 2.3.4).

4.2.6. Pass an objectivity evaluation administered by the Chief of Stan/Eval or designee based on the NAF approved SEE training and certification program. Objectivity evaluations can be administered by HHQ personnel IAW paragraph 2.4.2.5. **(T-3)**

4.2.7. Conduct a thorough pre-evaluation briefing and post-evaluation debriefing for the examinee and applicable cybercrew members on all aspects of the evaluation. **(T-3)**

4.2.8. Debrief the examinee's flight commander or operations officer on the results of the evaluation. As soon as possible, notify the examinee's squadron commander (or available supervision if the squadron commander cannot be reached) whenever Qualification Level 2 or 3 (Q2 or Q3) performance is observed (see paragraph 5.4). **(T-3)**

Chapter 5

CYBERCREW QUALIFICATION EVALUATIONS

5.1. General. The Cybercrew Stan/Eval Program utilizes cybercrew evaluations to ensure qualification of cybercrew members and standardization of operations.

5.2. Categories. Cybercrew qualification evaluations are divided into three categories, (Qualification (QUAL), Mission (MSN), and SPOT), each consisting of two structured phases, written and performance. (Exception: A SPOT evaluation may only consist of one phase, depending on its purpose.)

5.2.1. QUAL Evaluations.

5.2.1.1. Purpose. Ensure basic qualification in a CWS and/or cybercrew position.

5.2.1.2. Execution. All cybercrews will complete periodic QUAL evaluation in their primary assigned CWS cybercrew positions in accordance with lead command developed criteria described in paragraph 2.3.2.1 of this instruction **(T-3)**. QUAL evaluations may be combined with MSN evaluations IAW lead MAJCOM guidance.

5.2.2. MSN Evaluations.

5.2.2.1. Purpose. To ensure qualification to employ the CWS at the assigned cybercrew position in the accomplishment of the unit's operational and/or designated operational capability (DOC) statement missions.

5.2.2.2. Execution. All cybercrew members maintaining MR/CMR status (IAW AFI 10-1703, Vol 1) will complete a periodic MSN evaluation as specified in the applicable lead MAJCOM guidance. **(T-1)**

5.2.2.2.1. The MSN evaluation should reflect the type and difficulty of tasks required in fulfillment of the CWS operational and/or DOC statement missions.

5.2.3. SPOT Evaluations.

5.2.3.1. Purpose. Evaluate a specific event or requirement without intending to satisfy the requirements of a periodic evaluation and/or an initial evaluation.

5.2.3.2. Execution. A SPOT has no specific requisites, unless specified in lead MAJCOM guidance, but may be no notice (N/N).

5.2.3.2.1. An examinee may utilize a SPOT evaluation to update a QUAL/MSN evaluation expiration date provided all requirements for the QUAL/MSN are met.

5.2.3.2.2. Any qualifying event and/or evaluation not listed in paragraphs 5.2.1 through 5.2.3 should be documented as a SPOT evaluation.

5.2.3.2.3. Objectivity evaluations should be documented as a SPOT on the AF Form 4418.

5.2.4. Prefixes. The following prefixes should be used, when applicable, to further describe the evaluations listed in paragraphs 5.2.1 through 5.2.3:

5.2.4.1. Initial (INIT). The first evaluation of any type in a specific CWS cybercrew position.

5.2.4.2. Requalification (RQ). An evaluation administered to remedy a loss of qualification due to:

5.2.4.2.1. Expiration of a required periodic evaluation. Commanders will ensure that the recheck is IAW the guidance for that periodic evaluation. **(T-3)**

5.2.4.2.2. Loss of currency that requires a requalification evaluation (IAW lead MAJCOM guidance). In this case, use RQ SPOT for documentation. The certifying official directs the requalification criteria, which will as a minimum include those items for which the individual is not current.

5.2.4.2.3. A failed periodic evaluation. The certifying official directs the requalification criteria, which will as a minimum include those items for which the individual failed the evaluation.

5.2.4.2.4. Loss of qualification due to a commander-directed downgrade (see paragraph 5.10). The commander will direct the recheck criteria on the AF Form 4418.

5.2.4.2.5. Do not use the RQ prefix with a requalification following a failed INIT evaluation. No qualification was achieved, thus requalification is not possible.

5.2.4.3. No-Notice.

5.2.4.3.1. The N/N evaluation program provides commanders a sampling of daily cybercrew performance and an assessment of unit training effectiveness.

5.2.4.3.2. A N/N evaluation is one where the examinee is notified of the evaluation at or after the beginning of the cybercrew changeover.

5.2.4.3.3. A N/N cannot be combined with an INIT evaluation.

5.2.4.4. Simulator (SIM). An evaluation where the performance phase requisite is conducted in a simulator as defined in lead MAJCOM guidance.

5.2.4.5. Multiple Prefixes. More than one prefix may be used to describe an evaluation. If it is not obvious in the context of the evaluation, explain the applicability or purpose of any prefixes on the AF Form 4418 IAW Chapter 8.

5.3. Phases. QUAL and MSN evaluations consist of two structured phases, written and performance. Passing of the written phase is a pre-requisite for the beginning of the performance phase. SPOT evaluations may consist of one or both phases depending on their purpose.

5.4. Qualification Levels. Qualification levels are grades assigned to the overall evaluation. Individual phases are graded IAW Chapters 6 and 7 and are considered when determining the overall qualification level. Qualification levels are:

5.4.1. Qualification Level 1 (Q1). The member demonstrated desired performance and knowledge of safety, procedures, equipment and directives within tolerances specified in the grading criteria. This is awarded when no discrepancies were noted, and may be awarded when discrepancies are noted if:

5.4.1.1. The discrepancies resulted in no unsatisfactory (U) grades being given in any area(s)/subarea(s).

5.4.1.2. All discrepancies noted during the evaluation were resolved during the debrief of that evaluation.

5.4.1.3. Passed written exam with score of 90-100 on first attempt.

5.4.2. Qualification Level 2 (Q2). The member generally demonstrated desired performance and knowledge of safety, procedures, equipment and directives within tolerances specified in the grading criteria, but:

5.4.2.1. There were one or more area(s)/subarea(s) where additional training was assigned.

5.4.2.2. A non-critical area/subarea grade of U was awarded.

5.4.2.3. Passed written exam with score of 80 to <90 on first attempt.

5.4.3. Qualification Level 3 (Q3). The member demonstrated an unacceptable level of safety, performance or knowledge. The member is not qualified to perform cybercrew duties.

5.4.3.1. An area grade of U awarded in a critical area requires an overall Q3 for the evaluation.

5.4.3.2. Failed written exam with a score of <80.

5.4.3.3. Reference paragraph 7.7 for retest scoring information.

5.4.4. Exceptionally Qualified (EQ) Designation (Optional). An EQ designation may be awarded by the examiner when:

5.4.4.1. The examinee has demonstrated exceptional skill and knowledge in all portions of the evaluation.

5.4.4.2. The examinee has not failed any part and;

5.4.4.3. The examinee received a Q1 grade with no discrepancies on all areas/subareas.

5.4.4.4. The operator passed written exam with a score of 95-100.

5.5. Evaluation Criteria. Evaluation criteria define the performance standards expected of cybercrews in their accomplishment of the mission. These standards are the measurement against which crewmembers are evaluated to achieve and maintain their qualifications. Lead MAJCOM-provided guidance identifies areas/subareas required for evaluation completion and provides required evaluation criteria. Attachment 3 gives examples for evaluation criteria.

5.6. Requisites. Requisites are defined as that combination of written examinations, performance examinations, and other requirements identified in lead MAJCOM-provided guidance as required for an evaluation to be considered complete.

5.6.1. Lead MAJCOM-provided guidance specifies requisites for each cybercrew position and associated qualifications.

5.6.2. Units that direct additional requisites beyond those specified in the appropriate lead MAJCOM-provided guidance must document these within their unit instructions **(T-3)**.

5.6.3. For multiple qualifications, the evaluation of one requisite may count for separate evaluations provided the evaluations occur IAW the provisions of section 5.7.

5.6.4. Requisites that were valid for a failed examination remain valid.

5.7. Timing of Qualification Evaluations.

5.7.1. Expiration Date. Required periodic evaluations are defined in the respective lead MAJCOM-provided guidance; however, Commanders will ensure that they do not exceed the last day of the 17th month after the evaluation was successfully completed **(T-3)**.

5.7.2. Requirements before Permanent Change of Station (PCS)/Temporary Duty (TDY). If a periodic evaluation expires within three months after the proposed departure for a PCS to an assignment in the same mission type, or during an upcoming TDY, complete the required evaluation(s) before departing for either the PCS assignment or the TDY.

5.8. Failure to Pass a Positional Evaluation.

5.8.1. Requalification. If a member fails a positional evaluation, Commanders will ensure that a successful RQ is completed within 30 calendar days after the date of the first failure (e.g., for an evaluation on 20 June, complete the recheck by 19 July) **(T-3)**. For Air Reserve Component (ARC) units, Commanders will ensure that a successful RQ is completed within 90 calendar days after the date of the first failure **(T-3)**.

5.8.2. Restrictions. When called for by this instruction or deemed necessary in the judgment of the SEE, the SEE may recommend restrictions be imposed on the examinee until successful completion of assigned additional training and/or a recheck. The certifying official, or designated representative, makes the final determination.

5.8.2.1. Restrictions should address the specific phase of operation that requires supervision and the criteria for removal of the restrictions.

5.8.2.2. QUAL Evaluation: Place the examinee on supervised status (see paragraph 5.8.4) on the system in which the evaluation was administered. For specialized and/or multiple qualified cybercrew maintaining qualification for similar duty in multiple CWSs, lead MAJCOM-provided guidance may direct supervised status on all systems in which the individual maintains qualification.

5.8.2.3. MSN Evaluation: Place the examinee on supervised status (see paragraph 5.8.4) on the system in which the evaluation was administered.

5.8.3. Status Downgrade. Cybercrew members receiving a Q3 QUAL and/or MSN evaluation are non-mission ready (N-MR)/non-combat mission ready (N-CMR) IAW lead MAJCOM-provided guidance. Place cybercrew members receiving a failing score on a QUAL on supervised status.

5.8.4. Supervised Status.

5.8.4.1. If an examinee is placed on supervised status as a result of unsatisfactory performance or restrictions, the squadron commander will determine the type of supervisor (i.e., instructor or designated supervisor) based on lead MAJCOM-provided guidance **(T-3)**.

5.8.4.2. The certifying official determines the restrictions to be imposed on the member.

5.9. Failure to Complete an Evaluation within the Required Period.

5.9.1. If a member fails to complete an evaluation within the period listed in paragraph 5.7, the member loses the qualification covered by the evaluation and the restrictions of paragraph 5.8 apply.

5.9.2. Qualification may be re-established by administering a requalification evaluation or by completion of the delinquent evaluation. OG/CC or designee may approve waivers to preclude the re-accomplishment of completed requisites to complete the evaluation on a case-by-case basis.

5.10. Commander-Directed Downgrade. The certifying official may direct a downgrade (Q-/U) in a specific area/sub-area without disqualifying an individual. Additionally, a certifying official may direct a downgrade that either removes a qualification or completely disqualifies an individual. Downgrades may be directed without administering an evaluation using the following guidance:

5.10.1. For performance-related cases use for cause only (e.g., breach of weapon system discipline, safety, etc.). Incidents do not have to be directly observed by an examiner, but may be recommended by an examiner from any CWS/cybercrew specialty.

5.10.2. For non-performance-related cases involving lapses of judgment significant enough to cause a commander to lose confidence in the cybercrew member's ability to safely operate the equipment, do not use a downgrade or disqualification as a substitute for or in lieu of appropriate progressive disciplinary measures (e.g., Verbal Counseling, Letter of Counseling, Letter of Reprimand, Article 15, etc.). Consult with the supporting Staff Judge Advocate office for legal advice in these cases. Use in cases where such incidences directly affect the commander's confidence in the cybercrew member's ability to safely operate the equipment (e.g., lapse in judgment significant enough to cast doubt on the cybercrews decision-making abilities on the system).

5.10.3. For downgrades that either remove qualifications or completely disqualify an individual, the affected cybercrew will cease acting in the qualification(s) from which they have been downgraded effective with the date the commander initiated the downgrade. **(T-3)**

5.10.4. Commanders will ensure that downgrades are documented IAW paragraph 8.3.2. **(T-3)**

5.11. Multiple Qualifications. Lead MAJCOM-provided guidance addresses evaluations in multiple cybercrew positions.

5.11.1. Documentation. MAJCOMs may authorize certification in more than one CWS for crewmembers only when such action is authorized by command mission requirements and is economically justifiable. This authority cannot be delegated below the MAJCOM level, except for the lead MAJCOM, which may further delegate within its command, but not lower than wing commander. Document MAJCOM authority for multiple qualifications in the IQF.

5.11.2. QUAL Evaluations. All members must have a QUAL evaluation in each position **(T-2)**.

5.11.3. Failure to pass an evaluation. A downgrade resulting from a failure of a QUAL applies only to the specific position for which the evaluation was administered.

Chapter 6

CYBERCREW PERFORMANCE EXAMINATION PROGRAM

6.1. Purpose. The performance program measures the skills and abilities of a crewmember through observation of their performance in a specific cybercrew position.

6.2. General.

6.2.1. Performance examination management. Unit stan/eval will develop and maintain standard performance examination scenarios for each position IAW Attachment 5. **(T-3)**

6.2.2. Performance examination scenario reviews. Unit stan/eval will review all steps of the performance evaluations for accuracy, feasibility, and correct process steps semi-annually. **(T-3)**

6.3. Grading System.

6.3.1. A two-step grading system is used to evaluate and document crewmember performance.

6.3.1.1. In the first step, individual grades are assigned against each area and subarea of the evaluation criteria established for the appropriate cybercrew position.

6.3.1.2. In the second step, an overall qualification level is assigned based on a compilation of all individual area/subarea grades IAW Chapter 5.

6.3.2. Performance Areas/Subareas.

6.3.2.1. Areas/subareas have a two-tier (Q/U) grading system for critical areas/subareas or three-tier (Q/Q-/U) grading system for non-critical areas/subareas in accordance with the appropriate lead MAJCOM guidance. **(T-3)** Document discrepancies against the established areas/subareas.

6.3.2.1.1. Q indicates the examinee demonstrated both a satisfactory knowledge of all required information and performed cybercrew duties within the prescribed tolerances.

6.3.2.1.2. Q- indicates the examinee is qualified to perform the assigned area/subarea tasks, but requires debriefing or additional training as determined by the SEE. Deviations should not exceed the prescribed Q- tolerances, jeopardize safety, or be a breach of CWS discipline.

6.3.2.1.3. U indicates that performance was outside allowable parameters, thereby compromising safety; that deviations from prescribed procedures/tolerances adversely affected mission accomplishment; and/or that evaluated performance constituted a breach of CWS discipline.

6.4. Conduct of a Performance Evaluation.

6.4.1. The examiner grades the areas/subareas as necessary within NAF-approved evaluation criteria.

6.4.2. In addition to required areas/subareas, the examiner will grade any area/subarea observed during an evaluation that was incidental to the task(s) being performed and the examiner observed less than acceptable performance which could adversely impact operations or overall safety. **(T-3)**

6.4.3. Minor momentary deviations are acceptable, provided the examinee applies prompt corrective action and such deviations do not jeopardize safety. Consider cumulative deviations when determining the overall area/subarea grade.

6.5. Remedial Action. An examinee receiving an area/subarea grade of Q- or U requires debriefing and/or additional training, as determined by the SEE.

6.5.1. Debriefed Discrepancy. Examiners will explain the discrepancy to ensure that the examinee has gained the necessary knowledge or proficiency. **(T-3)**

6.5.2. Additional Training. Any training recommended by the examiner to remedy deficiencies identified during an evaluation.

6.5.2.1. May include self-study, use of a simulator, supervised operations on the "live" network, or operations in a range environment.

6.5.2.2. Commanders will ensure that the training is complete 30 days following the date of the discrepancy **(T-3)**. For ARC units, commanders will ensure that the training is complete within 90 calendar days after the date of the discrepancy. **(T-3)**

6.5.2.3. If a cybercrew member exceeds the allotted time for completion of additional training, the certifying official will review the situation, direct appropriate action, and document the circumstances on the AF Form 4420. **(T-3)**

6.5.2.4. Document additional training on the AF Form 4418.

6.5.2.5. Requires a SPOT evaluation of the area(s)/subarea(s) in which additional training was prescribed within 30 days of additional training completion. Document SPOT evaluation on a separate AF Form 4418.

6.6. Supervised Status Requirement. Place personnel who fail performance examination in supervised status until successful retesting is completed.

6.7. Re-Evaluation.

6.7.1. Unit stan/eval will administer an alternate examination upon completion of retraining, but no later than the last day of the first month following the date of the discrepancy. **(T-3)** Unit stan/eval should accomplish re-testing prior to the end of the crewmember's eligibility window. ARC units will administer an alternate examination within 90 calendar days after the date of the first failure. **(T-3)**

6.7.2. The authority to extend the time allowed to successfully complete the examination is the OG/CC.

Chapter 7

CYBERCREW WRITTEN EXAMINATION PROGRAM

7.1. Purpose. The examination program measures knowledge, procedures, and other information for effective operations through the administration of written, computer-based, or electronic examinations. Poor testing performance on examinations indicates areas requiring increased training emphasis.

7.2. General.

7.2.1. Examination Management. Unit stan/eval will develop and maintain a minimum of two different examinations for each position, or generate a unique test for each person requiring an exam. **(T-3)**

7.2.1.1. A closed-book exam is required as a prerequisite to a QUAL or MSN evaluation. An open book exam may also be administered as a prerequisite to a QUAL or MSN evaluation in conjunction with the closed-book exam. If both an open- and a closed-book exam are administered, the scores are considered separately when determining the overall qualification level. For example, if the examinee fails the closed-book exam on the first attempt, but scores 100% on the open-book, upon passing the closed-book exam the highest overall rating allowed is Q-2.

7.2.1.2. Unit stan/eval will change a minimum of 25 percent of the questions on each examination every calendar year. **(T-3)**

7.2.2. Examination Reviews. Unit stan/eval will review all MQFs and prepared exams for accuracy annually and after any changes in source documents. **(T-3)** If a complete review was accomplished due to a source document change, it may be annotated as the annual review.

7.2.3. Examination Security. Unit stan/eval will maintain positive control of all exams, applicable answer sheets, and associated computer-based/electronic media. **(T-3)**

7.2.4. Examination Question Sources.

7.2.4.1. Open Book Exams (Optional). Open book exams are derived from technical orders, manuals, handbooks, or instructions containing information pertinent to the operation and performance of the assigned mission. They cover information which may not require immediate recall or be regularly referenced.

7.2.4.2. Closed Book Exams (Required). Questions in closed book exams are derived from MQFs, and emphasize system knowledge, time-sensitive information, and information required to be immediately recalled for quick responses.

7.2.5. End-of-Course Examinations. Formal training units (FTU) administering USAF formal school courses listed in the *Air Force Education and Training Course Announcement (ETCA)* database (https://etca.randolph.af.mil/) may use end-of-course (EOC) examinations to fulfill the requirements of the open book and closed book requisite examinations.

7.2.5.1. The MAJCOM stan/eval responsible for the USAF formal training will coordinate with AF/A6CF to ensure the EOC examination meets the requirements of this instruction and applicable instructional supplements before awarding credit for requisite completion.

7.2.5.2. EOC examination test questions do not need to incorporate NAF-approved MQFs; however, all questions should reflect the latest changes to all systems and/or operational procedures and not conflict with any MQFs.

7.2.5.3. Grade all EOC examinations that fulfill the requirements of requisite examinations according to this AFI and appropriate lead MAJCOM guidance, and enter the results on the stan/eval qualification documentation.

7.3. Grading System.

7.3.1. The total number of questions on a written exam should be determined by the total number of areas graded within the appropriate lead MAJCOM guidance. The minimum passing grade for all stan/eval examinations is 80 percent.

7.4. Conduct of Written Examinations.

7.4.1. For open book exams, examiners will make available to examinees all source publications used to generate the exam. **(T-3)**

7.4.2. Unit stan/eval will leverage computer-based or electronic examinations when feasible.

7.4.3. Unit stan/eval will retain graded exam answer sheets/computer records until the stan/eval qualification documentation is completed.

7.5. Remedial Action. An examinee receiving a failing grade on a written examination requires debriefing and additional training (as determined by the SEE) and a retest. Notify the examinee's supervisor of the exam failure immediately.

7.5.1. The examiner should provide instruction concerning the missed test questions to ensure the examinee understands the areas/subareas that should be addressed. **(T-3)**

7.5.2. Remedial Training. The examinee will complete remedial training with the assistance of an instructor, as needed; remedial training may include self-study, use of a simulator, supervised operations on the "live" network, or operations in a range environment. **(T-3)**

7.5.2.1. The examinee will complete remedial training by the last day of the first month following the date of the discrepancy (e.g., for an evaluation on 21 February, remedial training must be accomplished by 31 March). **(T-3)** For ARC units, the examinee will complete remedial training within 90 calendar days after the date of the discrepancy. **(T-3)**

7.5.2.2. If a cybercrew member exceeds the allotted time for completion of remedial training, the certifying official reviews the situation, directs appropriate action, and documents the circumstances with a memorandum for record (MFR) to be included with the AF Form 4418. **(T-3)**

7.5.2.3. Document additional training on the AF Form 4418.

7.5.3. In the event of a second failure on an exam, notify the certifying official, who will direct required actions to be taken. **(T-3)** Do not administer further examinations until directed by the certifying official.

7.6. Supervised Status Requirement. Commanders will ensure that personnel who fail a requisite open book or closed book examination are placed in supervised status until successful retesting is completed. **(T-3)** For personnel who maintain multiple qualifications, supervised status resulting from failure of either an open or closed book examination applies only to the position for which the examination was administered.

7.7. Retest.

7.7.1. Unit stan/eval will administer an alternate exam upon completion of retraining, but no later than the last day of the first month following the date of the failure. **(T-3)** For ARC units, unit stan/eval will administer an alternate examination within 90 calendar days after the date of the first failure. **(T-3)**

7.7.2. The authority to extend the time allowed to successfully complete the examination is the OG/CC. However, if the eligibility window falls within 30 days, every effort should be made to re-examine prior to expiration.

7.7.3. Commanders will ensure that a person failing a written examination is afforded an adequate study period prior to re-examination. **(T-3)**

7.7.4. A person failing a written examination may not receive an overall qualification rating greater than Q2 after passing the retest.

Chapter 8

DOCUMENTATION

8.1. Scope. Administration of the Qualification Evaluation Program requires accurate and standardized documentation. The qualifications and authorizations for which a person is to be evaluated are determined from the unit certification document. The results of evaluations are recorded on AF Form 4418, which certifies the member's qualification.

8.1.1. Record the results of cybercrew evaluations on AF Form 4418 and the chronological history of evaluations for a member on AF Form 4420. Maintain these forms in the IQF.

8.1.2. The use of electronic forms is authorized, to include use of electronic signatures and wholly electronic IQFs IAW lead MAJCOM guidance. In all instances, computer-generated forms should include the same information/data as AF Forms as published on the USAF E-Publishing web site.

8.2. Electronic Database. Units are highly encouraged to use electronic database files for record keeping, trend analysis, printing of standard forms, etc. The lead MAJCOM will establish standards for archiving and assessment of electronic files. Units not using an electronic database will maintain hard-copy records in accordance with this instruction.

8.3. AF Form 4418, *Certificate of Cybercrew/Spacecrew Qualification*.

8.3.1. Purpose. Use the AF Form 4418 as the source document to record and verify the qualification of a cybercrew member on a CWS.

8.3.2. Completion of an AF Form 4418 is accomplished by three individuals; the examiner, a final approving officer, and the examinee. Exception: for an AF Form 4418 which documents a Commander-Directed Downgrade, only the commander, as the final approving authority, and the individual affected sign the form.

8.3.3. Use a separate AF Form 4418 for all positional phase rechecks.

8.4. AF Form 4420, *Individual's Record of Duties and Qualification*. The AF Form 4420 is an index providing pertinent information extracted from all the AF Forms 4418 accomplished for the member. A computer generated AF Form 4420 may be used as long as cumulative entries are retained.

8.5. Individual Qualification Folder (IQF). The IQF contains the source documents that constitute the history of certification for each member. The AF Form 4418 is the source document used to record certification of a member. A complete history of the AF Forms 4418 in an IQF is maintained on an accompanying AF Form 4420. Software applications capturing the same information are authorized provided the unit gains approval by the MAJCOM stan/eval office prior to use.

8.5.1. Electronic format IQFs are authorized provided proper security measures, backup capability, and sustainment plans are in place. If electronic IQFs are used, the Chief of Stan/Eval (or equivalent) will publish guidance on storage and layout. **(T-3)**

8.5.2. Maintaining IQF. Commanders will ensure that each member who is in a MR/CMR position has an IQF, which includes all AF Forms 4418 and 4420.

8.5.2.1. A stan/eval functional office, normally in the organization to which the individual is assigned or attached for operational duties, will maintain the IQF. **(T-3)**

8.5.2.2. HHQ personnel on active operational status may have their IQFs maintained by the stan/eval function at their assigned stations.

8.5.2.3. Maintain IQFs for personnel in inactive operational status within a collocated stan/eval office.

8.5.2.4. Describe IQF maintenance in a supplement to this instruction.

8.5.2.5. Individuals assigned or attached to other than USAF units may use the format of the service to which they are assigned/attached to document their history of qualification/ certification.

8.5.3. Contents of IQF. If the IQF is maintained as a hard-copy record, divide it into two sections:

8.5.3.1. Section I (left side). This section contains AF Form 4420.

8.5.3.1.1. Place AF Forms 4420 on top of Tab 1 in this section in chronological order with the most recent on top.

8.5.3.1.2. If used, file electronic storage media in Section I of the IQF.

8.5.3.2. Section II (right side). This section contains AF Forms 4418 and MFRs for all evaluations listed on the AF Form 4420 in Section I.

8.5.3.2.1. File AF Form 4418s in chronological order with the most recent on top. Individuals who maintain qualification in two or more positions in the same CWS will file AF Form 4418s in chronological order, without consideration of CWS or position. **(T-3)**

8.5.3.2.2. File MFRs documenting waivers and extensions on top of the affected AF Form 4418. When action is complete, incorporate the information contained in the MFR onto the affected AF Form 4418 under Examiner Remarks paragraph D, Additional Comments and remove the MFR from the IQF. File permanent MFRs documenting major discrepancies relating to qualification immediately above the latest affected AF Form 4418. In cases where the MFR is for other items than those found on the AF Forms 4418, they are filed in chronological order with AF Forms 4418. MFRs become a permanent part of the IQF only when the major discrepancy addressed by the MFR is *not* addressed or corrected by a later Form 4418.

8.5.3.2.3. File MFRs documenting major discrepancies of a particular AF Form 4418 on top of that AF Form 4418 regardless of the date the discrepancy is discovered.

8.5.3.2.4. File MFRs documenting similar discrepancies found on multiple AF Form 4418s on top of the latest affected AF Form 4418.

8.5.3.2.5. Copies of these source documents may be filed with other organizations for evaluation program management.

8.5.4. Review of IQF. Document the procedures on how to accomplish an initial review and how to implement the periodic review of IQFs in the supplemental guidance to this instruction.

8.5.4.1. Initial Review. The unit will review the IQF for all newly assigned members to establish their currency and qualification prior to their first mission, and document this review on the AF Form 4420. **(T-3)** Review previous AF Form 4420 entries to determine all applicable qualifications/certifications of the new assigned/attached member. The gaining unit commander will document acceptance of applicable qualifications/certifications on a new AF Form 4420 with "Initial Review" signed by the commander as the last entry. **(T-3)**

8.5.4.1.1. The unit commander is responsible for establishing the currency and qualification of the member as determined from the latest applicable documentation in sections I and II of the IQF. Following determination of the currency and qualification of the member, the unit maintaining the IQF is responsible only for documentation subsequently placed in the IQF.

8.5.4.1.2. If the IQF of HHQ personnel on active operational status is maintained by the stan/eval function at their assigned stations, that stan/eval function will also review the IQF prior to operations. **(T-3)**

8.5.4.2. Posting Review. The stan/eval function will review each AF Form 4418 when it is placed in the IQF to ensure accuracy and completeness **(T-2)**. This review will confirm that the eligibility period and qualification as documented are correct, all required evaluation events and requisites were accomplished within the eligibility period, and that the AF Form 4418 contains all signatures and initials within allotted time.

8.5.4.3. Periodic Review. The stan/eval function reviews all unit IQFs to confirm expiration dates used to track required qualification evaluations are the same as those listed in the IQFs. The stan/eval function will ensure that the interval between reviews does not exceed the qualification period window established by paragraph 5.7. Document the periodic review IAW instructional supplements. Periodic review of IQFs for personnel in inactive status is not required.

8.5.5. IQF Discrepancies. IQF Discrepancies include those on the AF Form 4418s and AF Form 4420.

8.5.5.1. Categories of Discrepancies. Discrepancies are categorized by their impact on qualification/certification and are either major or minor.

8.5.5.1.1. Discrepancies that alter the qualification/certification of the affected member are considered major (i.e., expired qualification).

8.5.5.1.2. Those discrepancies that do not alter the qualification/certification of the affected member are considered minor (i.e., typos, formatting, or misspellings).

8.5.5.2. Disposition of Major Discrepancies. Document major discrepancies on an MFR filed in Section II immediately above the affected AF Form 4418. Remove MFRs created to document late evaluations, Group CC waivers, etc., from the IQF once the information is incorporated onto the completed affected AF Form 4418 under examiner remarks paragraph D, Additional Comments. MFRs become a permanent part of the IQF only when the major discrepancy addressed by the MFR is *not* addressed or corrected by a later AF Form 4418.

8.5.5.3. Disposition of Minor Discrepancies. Document minor discrepancies on a non-permanent record as defined by supplements to this instruction. The record of minor discrepancies ensures standardization of AF Forms 4418, AF Form 4420, and member IQFs.

8.5.5.4. Corrections.

8.5.5.4.1. AF Form 4418. Because it is a source document, the AF Form 4418 may not be corrected by use of white-out/over-print or pen and ink alteration of the original document.

8.5.5.4.2. AF Form 4420. AF Forms 4420, not being source documents, may be altered without restriction to reflect the assignment of the affected member and the contents of Section II of the IQF.

8.5.6. Transfer of IQF. The losing unit will coordinate with the member and the gaining unit to transfer the IQF **(T-3)**. The IQF may be either hand-carried by the member or, in the case of digital or classified files, transmitted electronically or by appropriate secure means.

Chapter 9

ADDITIONAL PROGRAMS (CIF, CII, GO/NO-GO, TREND ANALYSIS, SEB)

9.1. Scope. This chapter provides guidance on additional programs administered by stan/eval.

9.2. Crew Information File (CIF). Units will establish and maintain a CIF **(T-3)**. The CIF is a library consisting of a current read file and publications. This library consists of volumes as listed in Table 9.1, in either hardcopy or electronic format **(T-3)**. All publications in the CIF should be current and complete.

Table 9.1. CIF Volumes

VOLUME	TITLE
VOLUME I	Table of Contents and Current Read File
VOLUME II (optional)	Publications—Air Force Directives/MAJCOM Supplements
VOLUME III (optional)	Publications—MAJCOM/NAF/Local Directives
VOLUME IV (optional)	Manuals/Checklists/Crew Aids/Technical Orders
VOLUME V (optional)	Safety Information – refer to Squadron safety program IAW AFI 91-202 and 91-203.

9.2.1. Current Read File. Volume I consists of a minimum of two parts to include an index (Part A) and current read files (Parts B and C (*Note:* Part C is optional)). MAJCOMs may add additional components to Volume I as appropriate.

9.2.1.1. Part A is a table of contents listing all material contained in CIF Volumes I through V.

9.2.1.2. Part B is the Current Read File of CIF messages. These messages contain information temporary in nature, directly pertinent to the safe conduct of operations, and must be read by all cybercrew members before operations **(T-3)**. Forward CIFs that contain system-related information to all using MAJCOMs.

9.2.1.3. Part C is the current read file that contains information temporary in nature but not related to the safe conduct of operations and not required to be read before operations.

9.2.2. Publications Library. Volumes II through IV, if used, consist of a CIF Functional Publications Library according to MAJCOM directives. See AFI 33-360 for basic library requirements.

9.2.2.1. All publications in the library should be current and complete. MAJCOMs may authorize units to withhold posting of information that does not apply based on system configuration.

9.2.2.2. Units will establish and maintain a table of contents for the publications library containing, at a minimum, a listing of basic publication numbers and short titles. **(T-3)** Publication dates, supplements, and changes are not required.

9.2.2.3. MAJCOMS may waive Volumes II-V requirements for special training units (i.e., 57 IAG).

9.2.2.4. File the CIF index and library IAW AFI 33-360, regardless of whether these are in hardcopy or electronic format.

9.2.2.4.1. If any part of the CIF library is maintained electronically and not specifically addressed above (or in AFI 33-360 and/or TO 00-5-1), units will ensure that the information is current and accessible for concurrent viewing by multiple cybercrew members. **(T-2)**

9.2.2.4.2. At a minimum, units will maintain the required index and location of electronic files in a hard-copy binder in the CIF library. **(T-3)**

9.2.2.4.3. Make documents in the CIF library available for deployments via either electronic or hardcopy means.

9.3. Stan/Eval Command Interest Items (CII). CIIs are a tool to train members on training deficiencies, new systems/procedures, or trends.

9.3.1. CIIs are emphasis items of existing procedures designed to mitigate or eliminate specific risks or trends. CIIs do not add to or amend established procedures. Base CIIs on analysis of risks and trends from a variety of sources. They may be issued by AFSPC, NAF, or units to address incidents, trends, deployed area operations, or potential problems with equipment/procedures. Only the issuing organization may rescind the CII.

9.3.1.1. The Chief of Stan/Eval, at the discretion of the command authority, establishes stan/eval CIIs.

9.3.1.2. CIIs should not be used as a routine message-passing vehicle; they should only be used to draw attention to changes or deficiencies in the certification and qualification processes.

9.3.2. When an item is designated for review and evaluation as a stan/eval CII, the stan/eval OPR assigns a CII number. The CII number is based upon the calendar year and numbered consecutively (i.e., I-NOSC CII 98-01, 26 NOG CII 99-01, or RAMSTEIN ESU CII 00-01). The OPR will then transmit a CII message to all affected subordinate units. **(T-3)** *Note:* CIIs may be published locally at any unit that maintains a stan/eval function.

9.3.3. The message that announces a new stan/eval CII includes applicable checklists and procedures, an expiration date, and a statement that identifies units and/or positions for which the CII is necessary. Publish CII messages and all pertinent information IAW the CEF requirements. Once the CII expires, all unit stan/eval functions shall incorporate the CII procedures into the permanent program wherever applicable. **(T-3)**

9.3.4. Do not establish a CII for a period longer than one year.

9.3.5. Commanders will ensure that all cybercrew positional and Crew Resource Management/Operational Risk Management (CRM/ORM) related CIIs are addressed in detail during turnover briefings for the duration of the CIIs. **(T-3)** Mission-related CIIs need only be briefed on those missions for which the CII is relevant.

9.3.6. Units will document CIIs in SEB minutes which should be maintained for historical purposes.

9.4. Go/No-Go Program. The Go/No-Go program ensures individual cybercrew members are current, qualified, or adequately supervised to perform operations and have reviewed CIF Volume 1, Part B prior to crew operations/shift change.

9.4.1. Units will establish a control system to ensure cybercrew members have completed all training and stan/eval items required for duty prior to shift turn over. **(T-3)**

9.4.2. The unit commander will appoint a scheduler who ensures Go/No-Go status is utilized for scheduling cybercrew members for operations.

9.4.3. The senior controller from the previous day/shift or unit commander's designated representative will certify the oncoming cybercrew prior to conducting operations. **(T-3)**

9.4.4. At a minimum, the Go/No-Go monitor will verify the following **(T-3)**:

9.4.4.1. The training items from AFI 10-1703, Volume 1 required for cybercrew duty.

9.4.4.2. The stan/eval testing items required for cybercrew duty from any unit supplement to this instruction.

9.4.4.3. Any mandatory training items not involving cybercrew duty but included at the discretion of the commander.

9.4.4.4. Currency on all CIF (Volume I, Part B) items. Accomplish an initial review and certification of all volumes prior to an individual's first operational mission. Assigned or attached cybercrew members on extensive absence from operational missions (90 days or more) will accomplish a complete review of all volumes and recertification prior to operations. **(T-3)**

9.4.5. Units will define and publish their control system in the unit supplement to this instruction. **(T-3)** Use the Go/No-Go procedures to document the review, certification, and acknowledgment of Volume 1, Part B information by assigned, attached, and visiting cybercrew members. Volume 1, Part C may be monitored by using Go/No Go procedures at unit discretion.

9.5. Trend Analysis Program. Trend analysis refers to the collecting of information to identify a pattern or predict future events. Each stan/eval function will establish a trend analysis program to identify, document, report, and recommend corrective action for all negative trends. **(T-3)** The trend analysis program is used to identify and track written, positional and periodic evaluation data for adverse trends. Group stan/eval will publish and define their trends program in a supplement to this instruction. **(T-3)**

9.5.1. Trend Analysis Monitor. The appointed trend analysis monitor will identify, track and record questions that are all incorrect (i.e. same question is not missed) or questions that are consistently missed (i.e. a question is missed by the majority) and all discrepancies or overt consistencies (lack of errors) on positional evaluations to create trend data. **(T-3)** The trend analysis monitor will compile and analyze the trend data on a quarterly basis to determine if any adverse, negative, or positive trends exist. **(T-3)**

9.5.2. Defining Trends. A positive trend is based on exceptional performance. An adverse or negative trend is defined as sustained poor, substandard performance by a group of members in a specific evaluation area over a period of time. The number of similar discrepancies required to constitute a trend varies depending upon the number of evaluations administered for a particular position.

9.5.3. Trend Responses. If a trend is identified by the above criteria, the trend analysis monitor will:

9.5.3.1. Notify the commander in writing through the Chief of Stan/Eval of the trend identification and recommend appointment of OPR. **(T-2)**

9.5.3.2. Research and recommend corrective actions for negative trends. **(T-2)**

9.5.3.3. Assign an Office of Collateral Responsibility (OCR). **(T-2)**

9.5.3.4. Identify the suspense date by which corrective actions should be in place. **(T-2)**

9.5.3.5. Follow-up on open trends to verify the actions taken to correct the trend. **(T-2)**

9.5.3.6. Ensure all trends are widely publicized in the unit using read files, bulletin boards, newsletters, or other means. **(T-2)**

9.5.3.7. Ensure trends are briefed at the SEB and included in minutes until closed. **(T-2)**

9.5.4. Closing Trends. Close trends only when a subsequent quarterly trend analysis indicates the adverse trend no longer exists.

9.6. Stan/Eval Board. An SEB is a forum convened at the group level to review and resolve stan/eval related issues. Examples include evaluation results, trends noticed during evaluations, stan/eval manning, waiver/extensions of evaluations, inspection results, and memoranda of agreement. Group stan/eval will publish and define its SEB program in a supplement to this instruction. **(T-3)**

9.7. Disposition of Documentation. Dispose of IQFs and other related material according to the AF Records Disposition Schedule (RDS), Table 36-12, Rule 02.00, and AF guidance concerning the protection of Personally Identifiable Information.

BURTON M. FIELD, Lt Gen, USAF
DCS Operations, Plans & Requirements

Attachment 1

GLOSSARY OF REFERENCES AND SUPPORTING INFORMATION

References

AFPD 10-9, *Lead Command Designation and Responsibilities for Weapon Systems*, 8 March 2007

AFPD 10-17, *Cyberspace Operations*, 31 July 2012

AFI 10-1703, Volume 1, *Cybercrew Training*, 5 April 2014

AFI 33-150, *Management of Communication Activities*, 30 November 2011

AFI 33-210, *AF Certification and Accreditation (C&A) Program (AFCAP)*, 23 December 2008

AFI 33-324, *The Air Force Information Collections and Reports Management Program*, 6 March 2013

AFI 33-360, *Publications and Forms Management*, 25 September 2013

AFI 36-2101, *Classifying Military Personnel (Officer and Enlisted)*, 14 June 2010

AFI 36-2201, *Air Force Training Program*, 15 September 2010

AFI 36-2605, *Air Force Military Personnel Testing System*, 24 September 2008

AFI 90-201, *The Air Force Inspection System*, 23 March 2012

AFI 91-202, *The US Air Force Mishap Prevention Program*, 5 August 2011

AFI 91-203, *Air Force Consolidated Occupational Safety Instruction*, 15 June 2012

AFMAN 33-282, *Computer Security (COMPUSEC)*, 27 March 2012

AFMAN 33-363, *Management of Records*, 1 March 2008

AFMAN 36-2236, *Guidebook for Air Force Instructors*, 12 November 2003

T.O. 00-5-1 *AF Technical Order System*, 1 October 2007

AF Records Disposition Schedule (RDS), located in AFRIMS (**https://www.my.af.mil/afrims/afrims/afrims/rims.cfm**)

Prescribed Forms

AF Form 4418, *Certificate of Cybercrew/Spacecrew Qualification*

AF Form 4420, *Individual's Record of Duties and Qualifications*

Adopted Forms

AF Form 847, *Recommendation for Change of Publication.*

AFTO Form 22, *Technical Manual Change Recommendation and Reply*

Abbreviations and Acronyms

ARC—Air Reserve Component

BMC—Basic Mission Capable

CIF—Cybercrew Information File

CII—Command Interest Item

CMR—Combat Mission Ready

CRM—Crew Resource Management

CWS—Cyberspace Weapon System

DO—Director of Operations

EQ—Exceptionally Qualified

EOC—End of Course

EPS—Evaluation Performance Standard

ETCA—Education and Training Course Announcement

FTU—Formal Training Unit

HHQ—Higher Headquarters

IAW—In accordance with

IMT—Information Management Tool

INIT—Initial Evaluation

INSTR—Instructor Qualification Evaluation

IQT—Initial Qualification Training

ISD—Instructional Systems Development

MA—Mission Area

MFR—Memorandum for Record

MQF—Master Question File

MQT—Mission Qualification Training

MR—Mission Ready

MSN—Mission Qualification Evaluation

N-BMC—Non-Basic Mission Capable

N-CMR—Non-Combat Mission Ready

N-MR—Non-Mission Ready

OCR—Office of Collateral Responsibility

OGV—Operations Group Stan/Eval

OPR—Office of Primary Responsibility

ORM—Operational Risk Management

PCS—Permanent Change of Station

PE—Performance Evaluation

Q—Qualified

RT—Recurring Training

RQ—Requalification evaluation

SAV—Staff Assistance Visit

SEB—Standardization and Evaluation Board

SEE—Standardization and Evaluation Examiner

SELO—Standardization and Evaluation Liaison Officer

SIM—Simulator Evaluation

SOP—Standard Operating Procedure

SPOT—Spot Qualification Evaluation

Stan/Eval—Standardization and Evaluation

TF—Training Folder

TO—Training Officer

TR—Training Requirements

TRS—Training Squadron

TTP—Tactics, Techniques, and Procedures

UQ—Unqualified

UTA—Unit Training Assembly

Terms

Additional Training.—This includes any training or action recommended by a SEE that must be completed following an evaluation. The TO determines training requirements (TRs) to correct deficiencies identified by stan/eval. Accomplish this training within 30 days (2 UTAs).

Attached Personnel.—This includes anyone not assigned to the unit but maintaining qualification through that unit. AFRC, ANG, and HAF augmented personnel are an example of attached personnel.

Basic Mission Capable. A cybercrew member who has satisfactorily completed IQT and MQT, but is not in fully—certified MR/CMR status. The cybercrew member must be able to attain MR/CMR status to meet operational taskings as specified in the applicable instructional supplements. This status is primarily for individuals in units that perform weapon system-specific operational support functions (i.e., formal training units, operational test and tactics development). BMC requirements will be identified in the appropriate lead MAJCOM-provided guidance.

Certification.—Designation of an individual by the certifying official (or his/her designee) as having completed required training and evaluation and being capable of performing a specific duty.

Combat Mission Ready.—A cybercrew member who has satisfactorily completed IQT and MQT, and maintains certification, currency and proficiency in the command or unit combat mission.

Commander Interest Item.—This is an operational area of concern designated by stan/eval functions for local units and all subordinate units. CIIs are intended to focus special attention on areas of concern and should be evaluated during formal stan/eval visits and positional evaluations.

Critical Task.—These are tasks where strict adherence to procedures and directives is mandatory; failure to satisfactorily accomplish this task directly impacts overall mission success.

Cyberspace Weapon System. A combination of one or more weaponized cyber—capabilities with all related equipment, materials, services, personnel, and means of delivery and deployment required for self-sufficiency.

Cybercrew Information File. A collection of publications and material determined by the MAJCOM and unit as necessary for day—to-day operations.

Downgrade. The downgrading of an individual from Q to UQ status due to failure of any positional evaluation, failure to complete a recurring evaluation by the scheduled date, or the unit commander determines the individual to be non—proficient.

Evaluation.—This includes positional and written examinations used to determine proficiency as prescribed by governing directives.

Formal Visit.—This is a visit conducted by the stan/eval function to subordinate units. The purpose is to evaluate the effectiveness of the unit stan/eval program and cybercrew and individual proficiency.

Individual Qualification Folder.—The IQF contains the basic documents that show the history of an individual's positional qualification. Only one IQF will be developed/maintained for an individual in accordance with paragraph 7.6. IQFs shall only be maintained by stan/eval.

Informal Visit.—This is an announced visit by the stan/eval function to subordinate units for proficiency training or for orientation.

Initial Qualification Training.—One or more courses covering system specific and/or positional specific training as a prerequisite to Mission Qualification Training (MQT).

Instructor.—An experienced individual qualified to instruct other individuals in mission area academics and positional duties. Instructors will be qualified appropriately to the level of the training they provide.

Master Question File.—A headquarters developed and published bank of questions for each crew position covering those aspects of the position that are common throughout the AF. Stan/Eval functions use the MQF in constructing written examinations that this instruction requires.

Mission Area.—A logical grouping by heading of position qualification criteria. Some MAs are broken into subareas to more closely break out large topics.

Mission Evaluation.—Qualifies a cybercrew member to employ the member's assigned system in accomplishing the unit's operational or DOC statement mission. Requires AF Form 4418 documentation.

Mission Qualification Training.—Training needed to qualify for cybercrew duties in an assigned cybercrew position for a specific CWS.

Mission Ready.—A cybercrew member who has satisfactorily completed IQT and MQT, and maintains qualification, currency and proficiency in the command or unit operational mission.

No—Notice Evaluation. An evaluation administered without prior notice or warning to test an individual's current skills.

Objectivity Evaluation—. The unit Chief of Stan/Eval (or his/her designated representative) gives this evaluation to unit SEEs to determine their ability to perform SEE duties. Document qualification as a SEE on an AF Form 4418 and designate the individual by letter upon completion of this evaluation.

Qualification.—Designation of an individual by the unit commander as having completed required training and evaluation and being capable of performing a specific duty.

Qualification Evaluation.—A written and/or positional evaluation conducted to check an individual's proficiency in performing operational duties or to let an examinee demonstrate to the SEE the academic knowledge and ability to do assigned position functions effectively. Types of qualification evaluations are Qualification (QUAL), Mission (MSN), and SPOT. Document qualification evaluations on AF Form 4418.

Recurring Training.—Academic and positional training required to maintain CMR and BMC status.

Requalification Evaluation.—An evaluation administered to remedy a loss of qualification due to expiration of a required periodic evaluation, loss of currency exceeding six months (as specified in applicable lead MAJCOM guidance), a recheck following a failed evaluation or a commander directed downgrade. Requires AF Form 4418 documentation.

SPOT Evaluation. Conduct this qualification evaluation to ensure correction of identified discrepancies or to spot check an individual's proficiency. A SPOT evaluation is normally limited in scope. It may be either a positional evaluation and/or a written examination. These evaluations may be either no—notice or given with prior coordination.

Standardization/Evaluation Examiner.—A SEE is an individual who has completed an objectivity evaluation and is designated to perform evaluation duties as specified by this instruction. SEEs must be current and qualified in the position they are evaluating.

Time Periods.—The following definitions are provided for interpretation of timing requirements specified in this instruction:

(a) Day— Unless otherwise specified, "day" means calendar days. When "work days" are specified, only count duty days. Do not count scheduled unit down days against this time limit.

(b) Month— The term "month" means calendar months, not 30-day periods.

Unit. For the purposes of this instruction, a unit is defined as a group/squadron/flight, I— NOSC squadron/detachment, or any operations section required to establish its own stan/eval program.

Unqualified. Previous CMR crewmembers whose CMR status has lapsed due to any of the reasons contained in AFI 10—1703, Volume 1, paragraph 2.4.

Attachment 2

MASTER QUESTION FILE

A2.1. Use the following information when developing questions for the Master Question File:

A2.1.1. Write questions for all knowledge level (A, B, C, D) tasks identified on the approved Master Training Task List. Questions may also be written covering the knowledge aspect of performance level (i.e. 2b, 3c, 4a etc…) tasks.

A2.1.1.1. Develop a minimum of two questions for each knowledge level task.

A2.1.2. Use AFMAN 36-2236, *Guidebook for AF Instructors*, Chapter 22 as a guide for question development.

A2.1.3. The preferred question format for MQFs is multiple-choice. Avoid true/false questions.

A2.1.4. Questions will include a reference for the correct answer. The reference will not be visible to the examinee when the question is administered. The reference will be used for validation as well as after-exam support in the event a question is challenged.

A2.1.4.1. Units will maintain a listing of all references used in exam questions to aid in determining if source material has changed when conducting annual exam reviews.

A2.1.5. The Group Chief of Stan/Eval will approve MQFs before submitting them to the NAF for final format review and approval.

Attachment 3

EVALUATION CRITERIA

A3.1. The following information provides assistance in developing evaluation criteria:

A3.1.1. Identify areas/subareas essential for mission accomplishment.

A3.1.2. Define the area criticality level (Critical (C), Major (M) or Minor (m).

A3.1.3. Group like tasks/subtasks and consolidate in a comprehensive area/subarea.

A3.1.3.1. Critical Area/Subarea. These are tasks that could result in mission failure, endanger human life, or cause serious injury or death. Critical areas/subareas have the greatest potential for extreme mission or personnel impacts and drive the most stringent training and evaluation program requirements. Critical areas/subareas apply to time-sensitive tasks or tasks that must be accomplished as expeditiously as possible without any intervening lower priority actions that would, in the normal sequence of events, adversely affect task performance/outcome.

A3.1.3.2. Major Area/Subarea. These are tasks deemed integral to the performance of other tasks and required to sustain acceptable weapon system operations and mission execution. Major areas/subareas drive significant training requirements.

A3.1.3.3. Minor Area/Subarea. These are rudimentary or simple tasks related to weapons system operations that by themselves have little or no impact on mission execution. Minor areas/subareas require the least stringent training requirements.

A3.1.4. For each area/subarea, identify the cybercrew position, Master Training Task List items included under the area/subareas, and the grading criteria for evaluation. Critical areas/subareas are graded either Q or U and Major/Minor area/subareas are graded with either a Q, Q- or U rating. Areas/subareas should also be marked with an "R" if required to be included on all evaluations. If not required on both a QUAL and MSN evaluation, precede the "R" with a Q for QUAL or M for MSN.

A3.1.5. Use the sample areas/subareas on the next pages as examples of required formatting only.

Table A3.1. (Sample) Critical Area Requirements

AREA 1: PERFORM EMERGENCY ACTION PROECEDURES (C) - R
MTTL TASK(S)
E01A: Execute Fire Response E01B: Execute Bomb Response E01C: Execute Severe Weather Response
EVALUATION STANDARD
Q. Obtained the correct checklist based on the scenario presented. Executed all required steps.
U. Failed to locate and/or utilize the appropriate checklist based on the scenario presented. Did not perform checklist steps correctly. Failed to meet one or more of the performance standards.

Table A3.2. (Sample) Major Area Requirements

UTILIZE COLLABORATION TOOLS (M)
MTTL Task(s)
B01A: Utilize Defense Connect Online B01B: Utilize mIRC Software
EVALUATION STANDARD
Q. Tool(s) utilized properly and in accordance with established standards. Knowledge on tool use was satisfactory.
Q-. Tool(s) utilized satisfactorily with minor errors in use not affecting overall mission execution. Knowledge on tool use was marginal.
U. Tool(s) utilized in an unsafe or inappropriate manner. Functions of tool(s) were unknown and/or could not demonstrate functions required of position. Knowledge on tool(s) use was unacceptable.

Table A3.3. (Sample) Minor Area Requirements

MODIFY SITUATIONAL AWARENESS BRIEFING (M) - QR
MTTL TASK(S)
B04A: Modify cybercrew changeover briefing
EVALUATION STANDARD
Q. All performance standards met.
Q-. Failed to meet one or more of the performance standards.
U. Performance standards were not met.

Attachment 4

STAN/EVAL BOARD MINUTES

A4.1. Note. The information below is an example of the minimum information a board should address. Use this template, although not all fields may necessarily be needed in each report.

Figure A4.1. Stan/Eval Board Minutes

MEMORANDUM FOR (SEE DISTRIBUTION)

FROM: (UNIT'S COMPLETE ADDRESS)

SUBJECT: STAN/EVAL BOARD MINUTES

1. Personnel Attending (name and organization)

2. Overview.

a. Manning. (Enter any stan/eval manning problems discussed or deviations from authorized manning. Record all current SEEs including attached HHQ and/or attached squadron SEEs.) Include any OG/CC designated additional OGV SEEs.

b. Summary.

(1) Evaluations. Report CWS evaluations by cybercrew position and type of evaluation (QUAL and MSN as outlined in the appropriate lead MAJCOM provided guidance). Include SPOT, N/N, and INIT INSTR evaluations, when applicable. Show qualification levels, sub-levels, and rates (rate = number of each type of test given divided by total given).

(a) Q1s

(b) Q2s

(c) Q3s

(d) Total evaluations for each cybercrew position

(2) Examinations. Report examination results by cybercrew position and type of examination (open book, and closed book.

(3) Waivers and Extensions. Identify all waivers and extensions as identified in this AFI.

(4) Trends. Identify new, continuing, and resolved trends. Where necessary, report corrective action as OPEN/CLOSED, the OPR(s) and any suspense date.

(5) Report progress toward achievement of no-notice requirements, if applicable.

c. Stan/Eval Program Inspections and Reviews (if applicable).

d. Cybercrew Publications. Review open AF Form 847s.

3. Old Business. Enter the disposition of any items left open at the last board meeting. If final action was taken on an item during the quarter, state the action taken and then close the item if closure is approved by the board chairman. If an item remains open, list the action taken since the last board. Findings from formal stan/eval inspections will be addressed and covered until they are closed out.

4. New Business. Enter all new business discussed during the board. The new business items are those included on the published agenda along with any unplanned items discussed.

5. Other: This is an optional paragraph that can be used as necessary.

6. Problems Requiring HHQ Assistance. Enter problems that, based on board resolution, require HHQ assistance. The assistance may be in any form (for example, staff assistance visit requests, clarification of directives, change of directives, and so forth).

                                        (SIGNATURE BLOCK)

Attachments:
1. Board Agenda
2. Weapon System Examiner Roster Reviewed
3. As Required

Attachment 5

PERFORMANCE EXAMINATION SCENARIO

A5.1. Use the following guidelines when developing a performance examination scenario:

A5.1.1. Unit stan/eval will develop and maintain a minimum of two scenarios per weapon system position.

A5.1.2. Scenarios will be mission based as compared to task oriented. The scenario should enable the examinee to move through events as they would normally when executing operational duties in the evaluated position.

A5.1.3. Scenarios will be as realistic as possible. Account for normal cybercrew structures and consider evaluating in a cybercrew setting rather than a one-on-one setting.

A5.1.4. Scenarios will reflect current approved evaluation criteria as well as current operations. As operations change, update evaluation criteria and scenarios as required.

A5.1.5. Scenarios will identify the area(s)/subarea(s) being evaluated, the supporting material/people required and any system configurations required.

A5.1.5.1. Develop supporting inject material at the same time as the scenario and label it in a manner that can be easily referenced in the scenario.

A5.1.6. Scenario developers should anticipate all possible responses (correct or incorrect) the examinee could take in response to injects and anticipate any possible safety or security concerns.

A5.1.7. The Group Chief of Stan/Eval will approve scenarios prior to their implementation.

A5.1.7.1. Unit stan/eval personnel will conduct a dry run on the scenario prior to submitting it for approval.

A5.1.7.2. The scenario will indicate the individual(s) involved in the scenario development, the date of dry-run and a signature block for the Group Chief of Stan/Eval.

A5.1.8. Re-certify scenarios at a minimum annually.

DEPARTMENT OF THE AIR FORCE
WASHINGTON, DC

AFI10-1703V3_AFGM2017-01

23 February 2017

MEMORANDUM FOR DISTRIBUTION C
MAJCOMs/FOAs/DRUs

FROM: SAF/CIO A6
1480 Air Force Pentagon
Washington, DC 20330-1480

SUBJECT: Air Force Guidance Memorandum to AFI 10-1703, Volume 3, *Cyberspace Operations and Procedures*

By Order of the Secretary of the Air Force, this Air Force Guidance Memorandum immediately changes Air Force Instruction 10-1703, Volume 3, *Cyberspace Operations and Procedures*, 6 May 2015. Compliance with this Memorandum is mandatory. To the extent its directions are inconsistent with other Air Force publications, the information herein prevails, in accordance with AFI 33-360, *Publications and Forms Management*. Ensure that all records created as a result of processes prescribed in this publication are maintained IAW Air Force Manual (AFMAN) 33-363, *Management of Records*, and disposed of IAW Air Force Records Information Management System (AFRIMS) Records Disposition Schedule (RDS).

As a result of the publication of AF Policy Directive 17-2, *Cyberspace Operations*, which supersedes AFPD 10-17, *Cyberspace Operations*, dated 31 July 2012; AFI 10-1703, Volume 3 is hereby renumbered as AFI 17-202, Volume 3. This Memorandum is a renumbering of AFI 10-1703 only; the title and content remain unchanged. I hereby direct the Office of Primary Responsibility (OPR) for AFI 10-1703 to conduct a special review in accordance with AFI 33-360 to align its content with AFPD 17-2. This will result in a rewrite or rescind action of AFI 10-1703.

This Memorandum becomes void after one year has elapsed from the date of this Memorandum, or upon incorporation by interim change to, or rewrite of AFI 10-1703, Volume 3, whichever is earlier.

WILLIAM J. BENDER, Lt Gen, USAF
Chief of Information Dominance and Chief
Information Officer

BY ORDER OF THE SECRETARY
OF THE AIR FORCE

AIR FORCE INSRUCTION 10-1703
VOLUME 3

6 MAY 2015

Operations

CYBERSPACE OPERATIONS
AND PROCEDURES

COMPLIANCE WITH THIS PUBLICATION IS MANDATORY

ACCESSIBILITY: Publications and forms are available for downloading or ordering on the e-Publishing website at **www.e-publishing.af.mil**

RELEASABILITY: There are no releasability restrictions on this publication

OPR: AF/A3CO/A6CO

Certified by: AF/A3C/A6C
(SES Peter E. Kim)
Pages: 11

This instruction implements Air Force (AF) Policy Directive (AFPD) 10-17, Cyberspace Operations, and establishes AF-wide basic procedures for the operation of cyberspace weapons systems approved by the Chief of Staff of the AF. This publication applies to all military and civilian AF personnel, members of the AF Reserve Command (AFRC), Air National Guard (ANG), and contractor support personnel in accordance with appropriate provisions contained in memoranda support agreements and AF contracts. The authorities to waive wing/unit level requirements in this publication are identified with a Tier ("T-0, T-1, T-2, T-3") number following the compliance statement. See AFI 33-360, Publications and Forms Management, Table 1.1 for a description of the authorities associated with the Tier numbers. Refer recommended changes and questions about this publication to the Office of Primary Responsibility (OPR) using the AF Form 847, Recommendation for Change of Publication; route AF Form 847s from the field through Major Command (MAJCOM) publications/forms managers to AF/A3C/A6C and AF/A6S. Ensure all records created as a result of processes prescribed in this publication are maintained in accordance with AF Manual (AFMAN) 33-363, Management of Records and disposed of in accordance with the AF Records Disposition Schedule (RDS) located in the AF Records Management Information System (AFRIMS).

1. General.

1.1. Overview. This instruction establishes procedures for personnel assigned to AF cyber weapon systems.

1.2. Specific Applicability. This instruction applies to all personnel who operate AF cyber weapon systems and/or their related equipment. Personnel performing cyberspace operational support or maintenance functions will comply with appropriate guidance in Methods and Procedures Technical Order (MPTO) 00-33A-1001, General Communications Activities Management Procedures and Practice Requirements, AFI 33-150, Management of Communications Activities, and/or AFI 36-2201, Air Force Training Program, as applicable. Cyberspace Combat Mission Ready (CMR) certification applies to all military and civilian personnel who have completed Undergraduate Cyber Training/Cyber Defense Operations Course, 39 IOS Initial Qualification Training (IQT) (if available) and Mission Qualification Training (MQT), have passed an evaluation and are certified by an appropriate certifying official. CMR requirements may apply to additional personnel at selected units at the direction of AF Space Command (AFSPC)/A3. (T-2)

1.3. Supplements. Major Commands (MAJCOMs)/Numbered Air Forces (NAF)/Wings/Groups/Squadrons may supplement this instruction to provide specific guidance to their aligned units in accordance with AFI 33-360. The Headquarters AF Directorates of Cyberspace Operations and Warfighting Integration (A3C/A6C) and Cyberspace Strategy and Policy (AF/A6S) will review and coordinate on all supplements to this instruction. Air Reserve Components (ARC) will provide a copy of any approved supplement to AF/A3C/A6C, AF/A6S, and AFSPC/A3.

1.4. Real-Time Operations & Innovation (RTOI). RTOI projects are operational rather than acquisition-related activities. The RTOI construct enables the USAF to generate tools and tactics in response to critical cyber needs at the fastest possible pace.

1.4.1. RTOI activities are specifically intended to satisfy urgent and short-term operational needs in response to:

1.4.1.1. Cyber Incidents/Events Category 0 thru 9, as outlined in the Chairman of the Joint Chief of Staff (CJCS) Instruction 6510.01F, Information Assurance (IA) and Support to Computer Network Defense (CND), and CJCS Manual 6510.01B, Cyber Incident Handling Program. Emergent threats and opportunities as determined by 24 AF/CC.

1.4.1.2. Newly discovered critical vulnerabilities not currently mitigated within the Air Force Enterprise network or capable of remediation by other means.

1.4.1.3. Critical cyberspace operational needs (both defensive and offensive), which 24 AF/CC has been tasked to fulfill or which have been identified through the conduct of daily operations.

1.4.2. RTOI complements the traditional acquisition framework, providing responsive technical solutions to urgent cyber needs which cannot be fulfilled by Rapid Acquisition (RA) or Foundational Acquisition methods. It is not intended to circumvent normalized operational and acquisition processes through informal relationships among the United States Cyber Command, the Armed Forces, the National Security Agency, and the Defense Information Services Agency. HQ AFSPC will develop specific policy for quick-reaction processes otherwise available for the rapid fielding of capabilities. (T-2)

1.5. Crew Responsibility. In conjunction with other governing directives, this instruction prescribes operations procedures for cyberspace weapons systems under most circumstances, but it is not a substitute for sound judgment or common sense, . As a general rule, except as noted in paragraph 3.5.1. or in guidance that states an action "must" or "shall" be carried out, operations or procedures not specifically addressed in this instruction may be accomplished if they enhance safe, effective mission accomplishment and are approved for execution by appropriate command authorities.

1.6. Waivers. Unless otherwise specified, AFSPC/A3I is the waiver authority for this instruction; this authority may be delegated to the wing commander level within AFSPC, but no lower.

1.6.1. Waiver requests which must be approved by HQ AFSPC/A3I will be appropriately classified and submitted in memo or message format to the 24 AF Operations Directorate (24 AF/A3/5) via channels appropriate to the level of classification; classified requests should be submitted to **24af.a3@lackland.af.smil.mil**, with copies to HQ AFSPC/A3I (**afspc.a3i.wf@afspc.af.smil.mil**) and HQ USAF/A3C/A6C (**usaf.pentagon.saf-cio-a6.mbx.a6c-a3c-workflow@mail.mil**). 24AF/A3/5 will recommend approval or disapproval; approved waiver requests will be forwarded to AFSPC/A3I for final approval. Each waiver request will include, at a minimum, the following information:

1.6.1.1. The specific requirement to which the waiver request responds.

1.6.1.2. Full justification/rationale for the waiver request.

1.6.1.3. The proposed waiver expiration date/time.

1.6.2. Approved waivers are valid for a maximum of one year from the effective date.

1.6.3. ARC units will forward waiver requests which cannot be granted at the wing commander level through command channels to the applicable MAJCOM Operations Division (e.g., ANG/A3C or AFRC/A3), for approval. Approved waivers are valid for a maximum of one year from the effective date. Provide information copies of approved waivers to AF/A3C/A6C, AFSPC/A3, and the ARC MAJCOM OPRs.

1.7. Changes and Clarifications. The HQ AF Director of Cyberspace Strategy and Policy (AF/A6S) has overall authority for administration of this instruction.

1.7.1. Recommend changes to this publication using AF Form 847. Coordinate and route AF Forms 847 through the unit's chain of command to AFSPC/A3I, **afspc.a3i.workflow@us.af.mil**, which will forward approved change proposals to AF/A6SS, 1480 Air Force Pentagon, Washington, DC, 20330-1480 (or via electronic message to AF/A6S Workflow, **usaf.pentagon.saf-cio-a6.mbx.a6s-workflow@mail.mil**), for final review and approval.

1.7.2. Process requests for clarification via memorandum or message to AFSPC/A3I through 24 AF/A3/5, **24af.a3@us.af.mil.** 24 AF will provide the NAF position prior to forwarding.

1.7.2.1. If a clarification request was initiated by telephone, the submitting unit will follow up in writing within one working day. (T-3)

1.7.2.2. AFSPC/A3I will route the response back to the requestor through 24 AF/A3/5.

2. Mission Planning.

2.1. Responsibility. Individual crews, unit operations, and intelligence functions jointly share responsibility for mission planning. The crew commander/senior crew member is ultimately responsible for all aspects of mission planning to include complying with command guidance. Unit commanders may establish weapon system specific mission planning requirements but will ensure an appropriate level of mission planning is conducted prior to each mission. (T-1)

2.2. Procedures. Effective mission accomplishment requires thorough mission planning and preparation. Failures in execution often result from poor mission preparation, therefore units will conduct thorough planning prior to every mission. General mission planning considerations are addressed in AFTTP 3-1, General Planning, and CWO specific planning consideration can be found in AFTTP 3-1, Cyber Warfare Operations, or other weapon system specific AFTTP 3-1 volumes. While not directive, these manuals are useful in ensuring adequate mission planning and employment. (T-1)

2.2.1. Units will accomplish sufficient planning to ensure successful mission accomplishment for all phases of operations. The mission commander/senior crew member will use the Plan-Brief-Execute-Debrief (PBED) process for mission planning. At a minimum, mission planning will include mission objectives, expected threats (identity and counter-tactics), weapons delivery, cancel/abort/rollback criteria and/or contingency plans, Rules of Engagement (ROE), Risk Management (RM), lessons learned and applicable Special Instructions (SPINS). (T-2)

2.2.2. Unit staff will provide crews sufficient time and resources to accomplish crew mission planning and mission briefing. Mission planning must be accomplished by members who understand the capabilities and limitations of their weapon system, in a realistic training and/or mission rehearsal environment. Unit staff will ensure other activities, such as recurring academic training, training device periods, additional duties, etc., do not interfere with time allotted for mission planning and crew mission briefing. The crew commander/senior crew member is ultimately responsible for the proper conduct of mission planning and must ensure sufficient time and materials are available to effectively plan the mission. (T-2)

2.2.3. Crew substitutions require approval by unit operations officer or higher. Crew substitutions may be made as long as the substitute crewmember is thoroughly briefed and understands all aspects of the mission. (T-3)

2.3. Crew Mission Planning. Detailed crew mission planning helps ensure mission objectives are understood by all crew members and an effective plan is developed to achieve those objectives. In preparation for and prior to each sortie, crews will take tactical objectives provided by higher headquarters organizations through tasking orders and create tactical tasks for execution in the next sortie.

2.3.1. All crew members must be present during shift change or sortie briefing unless specifically excused by the squadron operations officer or higher authority. The crew commander/senior crew member will direct detailed mission planning, including procedures to employ. Crew commander/senior crew member will review all crew and crewmember training requirements and currency data to the maximum extent possible;

review crew and weapon system restrictions for each activity planned and plan an alternate mission/activity in the event equipment failure prevents accomplishing the primary mission. (T-3)

2.3.2. The crew commander/senior crew member is ultimately responsible for ensuring the adequacy and completeness of all mission data and resources and must make risk determinations to cancel or abort missions. The crew commander/senior crew member must ensure crew substitutions are made in time for the substitute crewmember(s) to be thoroughly briefed and familiar with the applicable mission data available and to rehearse with the rest of the crew in realistic range/training facilities, as required. (T-2)

2.4. Weapons and Tactics. Weapons and Tactics personnel will support the employment of current/effective TTPs, the planning/briefing/execution/debriefing of missions, and development of lessons learned. (T-2)

2.5. Intelligence and Threat Study. During mission planning, crews will receive a current intelligence briefing which will include detailed briefings on current adversary activity, threat type and capabilities. Crews will also review applicable TTPs and implement in accordance with mission requirements. (T-2)

3. **Normal Operations.**

3.1. Crew Logs. The crew log is the official record of events that occur during a crew shift or sortie (live or simulated). The purpose of the log is to maintain an accurate and detailed record of all significant events, including any deviations from guidance in this Instruction pertaining to operations occurring during each crew shift. Of primary importance are events that may result in subsequent investigations. At a minimum, crew logs will include identification of on-duty personnel, major operational activities, significant communications, major system degradations and other abnormal system responses. Maintain crew logs for one year to provide historical reference for mission operations. (T-3)

3.2. Crew Information File (CIF). The CIF provides information essential to the conduct of normal operations and response to emergency conditions. The CIF centralizes significant, time-sensitive issues and ensures procedures are disseminated to operations personnel. All crew members are required to review the CIF and acknowledge completion prior to beginning crew duties. Refer to AFI 10-1703, Volume 1, Cybercrew Training, for information on the structure and content of the CIF. (T-3)

3.3. Crew Shift/Mission Briefing. A successful mission briefing covers objectives tasked by higher headquarters, assigns tactical tasks to achieve those objectives, and ensures all crew members understand the plan.

3.3.1. The crew commander/senior crew member will conduct a crew mission briefing and rehearsals as necessary for all missions. When rehearsals confirm mission feasibility, the responsible commander approves the mission plan and authorizes execution. Crews will practice, mission plan and modify operational details according to rehearsal results. (T-3)

3.3.2. A crew member excused from the mission briefing, or substituted following the briefing, must receive a detailed briefing from the crew commander/senior crew member and be afforded an opportunity to rehearse his/her role with other crewmembers, as required. (T-3)

3.4. Shift/Mission Debriefing. The crew commander/senior crew member will lead a thorough mission debrief for every mission. The mission debrief will cover the following at a minimum: whether tasks and objectives were met, lessons learned, and learning points. (T-3)

3.5. Checklists, Local Procedures, and Crew Aids.

3.5.1. Crew members will strictly adhere to all checklists in a technical order (TO), all unit generated checklists or other higher headquarters (HHQ) directives. (T-2)

3.5.2. 24 AF/A3 will generate guidance to cover actions not addressed in a TO or other directives. (T-2)

3.5.3. Units may develop local procedures specific to their mission when operations fall outside existing TOs and HHQ guidance. Local procedures will not be used to re-create or consolidate existing technical data or HHQ guidance. (T-3)

3.5.4. Crew members may develop local crew aids such as charts, question banks, guides or other visual aids and processes to bolster proficiency, enhance changeover briefings and to ensure comprehensive tasks are completed correctly. However, these aids will not override or be used in lieu of TOs and other directives. The squadron commander will review and recommend approval/disapproval of all locally developed crew aids. Local crew aids will be approved by the Group commander or his/her designee. (T-3)

3.5.5. Briefing Guides. Units will develop local briefing guides to ensure all necessary items are covered prior to each mission. Group-level Stan/Eval, or designated stan/eval entity, will determine minimum requirements for these guides and ensure standardization. (T-3)

3.5.5.1. Guides will contain procedural guidance addressing mission accomplishment with abnormal/degraded/inoperative equipment. (T-3)

3.5.5.2. Guides will contain other information deemed necessary by individual units, i.e., local training procedures, and procedures for notifying maintenance personnel of equipment discrepancies. (T-3)

4. Operational Tests and Exercises. Exercising, testing and evaluating the crew force is necessary to maintain proficiency; however, exercises and tests also provide important data needed to validate the operation of the weapon system. (T-3)

4.1. During an exercise or test, crewmembers will and follow established operating procedures, AFIs, and governing publications with the understanding that exercise and tests are an avenue to try new TTPs and capabilities. RM should be performed at all levels to mitigate any risk. (T-3)

4.2. Exercises and tests will not jeopardize real-world missions. Real-world emergencies or priorities may require a crew to withdraw from a test or exercise. The crew commander/senior crew member will coordinate with the unit commander or operations officer and all other participating agencies to cancel, postpone or withdraw from a test or exercise. (T-3) When priority actions are complete, the crew may be permitted to resume participation as approved by appropriate authorities.

5. Crew Force Management.

5.1. Crew Rest, Fatigue Management and Duty Limitations. This section prescribes mandatory crew rest and maximum duty periods (DP) for all personnel who operate AF cyberspace weapon systems. Basic guidance for fatigue management strategies and waiver authority procedures are also addressed. (T-3)

5.1.1. The normal crew DP should not exceed 12 hours. (T-3)

5.1.2. When authorized by the appropriate group commander, the crew commander/senior crew member may extend the maximum DP up to two hours to compensate for unplanned mission delays, provided the mission requirements justify the increased risk. Extended DP must be annotated in the mission log, at a minimum detailing authorizing official (i.e., group commander or designated representative) and crew members affected. Mission or environmental needs requiring longer than a 14 hour DP require wing commander approval (may be delegated to OG/CC or equivalent). (T-3)

5.1.3. Regardless of authorized DP, the crew commander/senior crew member will restrict duty time, extend crew rest periods, notify squadron leadership to generate alternate crews, or terminate a mission if safety may be compromised by fatigue factors. (T-3)

5.1.4. DP begins when a crew member reports for a mission/sortie, briefing, or other official duty and ends with the completion of the mission debrief. (T-3)

5.1.5. The crew rest period is a 10-hour non-duty period before the DP begins. Its purpose is to ensure the crew member is adequately rested before performing a cyberspace mission or mission-related duties. Crew rest is free time, and includes time for meals, transportation and the opportunity for eight hours of uninterrupted sleep. (T-3)

5.1.6. Crew rest is compulsory for any crew member prior to performing any crew duty on any cyber weapon system. (T-3)

5.1.7. Each crew member is individually responsible to ensure he or she obtains sufficient rest during crew rest periods. (T-3)

5.1.8. Any official business or duty that requires the active participation of a crew member, not during the DP, interrupts the crew rest period. This includes official business conducted via telephone or other electronic means. If crew rest is interrupted so that the individual cannot get an opportunity for at least eight hours of uninterrupted sleep, the individual must be afforded the opportunity for at least eight more hours of uninterrupted sleep plus reasonable time to dress, eat, travel, etc. Intentional crew rest interruptions shall only be made under the most exceptional circumstances. The individual must consider unofficial interruptions so that the intent of this section is met. If crew rest is interrupted, individuals will inform a supervisor and remove themselves from the mission schedule, when necessary. (T-3)

5.1.9. Exceptions to the 10-Hour Minimum Crew Rest Period. For continuous operations when basic crew DPs are greater than 12 but less than 14 hours, subsequent crew rest may be reduced proportionally to a minimum of 10 hours to maintain a 24-hour work/rest schedule. (T-3)

5.1.10. Continuous operations is defined as two or more consecutive DPs of at least 12 hours duration separated by minimum crew rest. (T-3)

5.1.11. The 10-hour crew rest exception shall only be used to keep crews in 24hour clock cycles, not for scheduling convenience and will not be sustained for more than 72 hours. (T-3)

5.1.12. Any reduction from 10 hours crew rest requires pre-coordination for transportation, meals and quarters as necessary so crewmembers are provided an opportunity for at least eight hours of uninterrupted sleep. (T-3)

5.1.13. Crew members will not perform cyberspace mission duties within 12 hours of consuming alcohol or other intoxicating substances, or while impaired by its after effects. (T-3)

5.2. Crew Scheduling. Crew scheduling will be accomplished in accordance with crew rest limitations provided in this guidance. (T-3)

5.2.1. Maintain crew integrity to the maximum extent possible.

5.2.2. Units should attempt to provide all crewmembers a stable schedule using a standard rotation for 24/7 crews to the maximum extent possible.

5.2.3. Operations Scheduling. Operations schedulers will publish, post and monitor schedules for the crew force and initiate changes to the schedules based on tracking of qualifications, certifications, restrictions and other factors as required to meet mission objectives. (T-3)

5.2.3.1. Operations schedulers will make schedule change notifications within 24 hours for changes that take effect within the next 72 hours. Make notifications as soon as practical after the change is official, but not later than 12 hours prior to the scheduled event time. (T-3)

6. Operations Review Board (ORB). MAJCOMs/NAFs will establish an ORB process for conducting investigations to determine the cause of any mission failures or significant events, including abnormal system responses or trends. If the initial analysis reveals the incident is outside the purview of the affected Wing, then the parent MAJCOM may request ORB support from HQ AFSPC. In cases where the responsible organization does not have the required expertise, the MAJCOM can request that expertise through HQ AFSPC. Exceptions can be worked on a case by case basis through MAJCOM to MAJCOM interaction, with appropriate support from all interested parties. Examples of circumstances requiring an ORB include: Major system degradation, indications of erroneous system response/procedures with significant mission impact and significant events where the cause cannot be determined by initial assessment or when corrective action is beyond minimal retraining or minor procedural changes. A significant, abnormal system response may include major hardware or software anomalies, safety violations, or security deficiencies.

TOD D. WOLTERS, Lt Gen, USAF
DCS, Operations, Plans & Requirements

Attachment 1

GLOSSARY OF REFERENCES AND SUPPORTING INFORMATION

References

National Military Strategy for Cyberspace Operations, December, 2006

DoDD O-3600.01, Information Operations, 2 May 2013

DoDD O-8530.1, Computer Network Defense (CND), 8 January 2001

DoDI O-8530.2, Support to Computer Network Defense (CND), 9 March 2001

Joint Publication 3-12, Cyberspace Operations, 5 February 2013

CJCSI 6510.01F, Information Assurance (IA) and Support to Computer Network Defense (CND), 9 February 2011

CJCSM 6510.01B, Cyber Incident Handling Program, 10 July 2012

AF Doctrine Annex 3-12, Cyberspace Operations, 15 July 2010, with Change 1, 30 November 2011

AFPD 10-17, Cyberspace Operations, 31 July 2012

AFI 10-710, Information Operations Condition (INFOCON), 10 August 2006

AFI 10-1701, Command and Control for Cyberspace Operations, 5 March 2014

AFI 10-1703V1, Cybercrew Training, 2 April 2014

AFI 33-360, Publications and Forms Management, 25 September 2013.

AFI 91202, The US Air Force Mishap Prevention Program, 5 August 2011

AFMAN 33-363, Management of Records, 1 March 2008

AFTTP 3-1, Tactical Employment Cyber Warfare Operations, 26 Apr 12

AFTTP 3-1, General Planning, 6 Feb 14

Methods and Procedures Technical Order (MPTO) 00-33A-1001, *General Communications Activities Management Procedures and Practice Requirements.*

TASKORD 14-005, Operation COBALT NEEDLE (OCN), 8 Apr 14

Adopted Forms

AF Form 847, *Recommendation for Change of Publication*

Abbreviations and Acronyms

AF—Air Force

AFI—Air Force Instruction

AFPD—Air Force Policy Directive

AFRC—Air Force Reserve Command

AFSPC—Air Force Space Command

AFTTP—Air Force Tactics, Techniques, and Procedures

ANG—Air National Guard

ARC—Air Reserve Component

C2—Command and Control

CIF—Crew Information File

CJCSI—Chairman, Joint Chiefs of Staff Instruction

CJCSM—Chairman, Joint Chiefs of Staff Manual

CMR—Combat Mission Ready

CND—Computer Network Defense

DoD—Department of Defense

DoDD—Department of Defense Directive

DoDI—Department of Defense Instruction

DP—Duty Period

HQ—Headquarters

IMSC—Installation and Mission Support Center

IQT—Initial Qualification Training

ISR—Intelligence, Surveillance, and Reconnaissance

JP—Joint Publication

MAJCOM—Major Command

MPTO—Methods and Procedures Technical Order

MQT—Mission Qualification Training

OC—Operations Center

OPR—Office of Primary Responsibility

RM—Risk Management

RTOI—Real-Time Operations and Innovation

SA—Situational Awareness

SPINs—Special Instructions

TO—Technical Order

USAF—United States Air Force

Terms

Cyberspace Operations.—The employment of cyberspace capabilities where the primary purpose is to achieve objectives in or through cyberspace. (JP 3-12)

Information Assurance (IA).— Measures that protect information and information systems by ensuring their availability, integrity, authentication, confidentiality, and nonrepudiation.

Network Operations (NetOps).— Activities conducted to operate and defend the Global Information Grid. (JP 6-0)

Sortie.— A cyber sortie (combat or training) constitutes the actions an individual cyberspace force package takes to accomplish a tasked mission. The base unit for a sortie is a cyberspace force package. A cyberspace force package completes a single sortie when it comes "off station" or the tactical commander declares a "knock it off". Missions may require multiple cyberspace force packages to conduct multiple sorties in order to accomplish mission objectives. (TASKORD 14-005)

Cybersecurity Titles Published by 4th Watch Publishing Co.

NIST SP 500-288 Specification for WS-Biometric Devices (WS-BD)
NIST SP 500-291 V2 NIST Cloud Computing Standards Roadmap
NIST SP 500-292 NIST Cloud Computing Reference Architecture
NIST SP 500-293 V1 & V2 US Government Cloud Computing Technology Roadmap
NIST SP 500-293 V3 US Government Cloud Computing Technology Roadmap
NIST SP 500-299 NIST Cloud Computing Security Reference Architecture
NIST SP 500-304 Data Format for the Interchange of Fingerprint, Facial & Other Biometric Information
NIST SP 800-12 R1 An Introduction to Information Security
NIST SP 800-16 R1 A Role-Based Model for Federal Information Technology/Cybersecurity Training
NIST SP 800-18 R1 Developing Security Plans for Federal Information Systems
NIST SP 800-22 R1a A Statistical Test Suite for Random and Pseudorandom Number Generators for Cryptographic Applications
NIST SP 800-30 Guide for Conducting Risk Assessments
NIST SP 800-31 Intrusion Detection Systems
NIST SP 800-32 Public Key Technology and the Federal PKI Infrastructure
NIST SP 800-34 R1 Contingency Planning Guide for Federal Information Systems
NIST SP 800-35 Guide to Information Technology Security Services
NIST SP 800-36 Guide to Selecting Information Technology Security Products
NIST SP 800-37 R2 Applying Risk Management Framework to Federal Information
NIST SP 800-38 Recommendation for Block Cipher Modes of Operation
NIST SP 800-38A Addendum Block Cipher Modes of Operation: Three Variants of Ciphertext Stealing for CBC Mode
NIST SP 800-38B Block Cipher Modes of Operation: The CMAC Mode for Authentication
NIST SP 800-38C Block Cipher Modes of Operation: The CCM Mode for Authentication and Confidentiality
NIST SP 800-38D Block Cipher Modes of Operation: Galois/Counter Mode (GCM) and GMAC
NIST SP 800-38E Block Cipher Modes of Operation: The XTS-AES Mode for Confidentiality on Storage Devices
NIST SP 800-38F Block Cipher Modes of Operation: Methods for Key Wrapping
NIST SP 800-38G Block Cipher Modes of Operation: Methods for Format-Preserving Encryption
NIST SP 800-39 Managing Information Security Risk
NIST SP 800-40 R3 Guide to Enterprise Patch Management Technologies
NIST SP 800-41 Guidelines on Firewalls and Firewall Policy
NIST SP 800-44 V2 Guidelines on Securing Public Web Servers
NIST SP 800-45 V2 Guidelines on Electronic Mail Security
NIST SP 800-46 R2 Guide to Enterprise Telework, Remote Access, and Bring Your Own Device (BYOD) Security
NIST SP 800-47 Security Guide for Interconnecting Information Technology Systems
NIST SP 800-48 Guide to Securing Legacy IEEE 802.11 Wireless Networks
NIST SP 800-49 Federal S/MIME V3 Client Profile
NIST SP 800-50 Building an Information Technology Security Awareness and Training Program
NIST SP 800-52 R1 Guidelines for the Selection, Configuration, and Use of Transport Layer Security (TLS) Implementations
NIST SP 800-53 R5 Security and Privacy Controls for Information Systems and Organizations
NIST SP 800-53A R4 Assessing Security and Privacy Controls
NIST SP 800-54 Border Gateway Protocol Security
NIST SP 800-56A R3 Pair-Wise Key-Establishment Schemes Using Discrete Logarithm Cryptography
NIST SP 56B R 1 Recommendation for Pair-Wise Key-Establishment Schemes Using Integer Factorization Cryptography
NIST SP 800-56C R1 Recommendation for Key-Derivation Methods in Key-Establishment Schemes - Draft
NIST SP 800-57 R4 Recommendation for Key Management
NIST SP 800-58 Security Considerations for Voice Over IP Systems
NIST SP 800-60 Guide for Mapping Types of Information and Information Systems to Security Categories
NIST SP 800-61 R2 Computer Security Incident Handling Guide
NIST SP 800-63-3 Digital Identity Guidelines
NIST SP 800-63a Digital Identity Guidelines - Enrollment and Identity Proofing
NIST SP 800-63b Digital Identity Guidelines - Authentication and Lifecycle Management
NIST SP 800-63c Digital Identity Guidelines- Federation and Assertions
NIST SP 800-64 R2 Security Considerations in the System Development Life Cycle
NIST SP 800-66 Implementing the Health Insurance Portability and Accountability Act (HIPAA) Security Rule
NIST SP 800-67 R2 Recommendation for Triple Data Encryption Algorithm (TDEA) Block Cipher - Draft
NIST SP 800-70 R4 National Checklist Program for IT Products
NIST SP 800-72 Guidelines on PDA Forensics
NIST SP 800-73-4 Interfaces for Personal Identity Verification
NIST SP 800-76-2 Biometric Specifications for Personal Identity Verification
NIST SP 800-77 Guide to IPsec VPNs
NIST SP 800-79-2 Authorization of Personal Identity Verification Card Issuers (PCI) and Derived PIV Credential Issuers (DPCI)
NIST SP 800-81-2 Secure Domain Name System (DNS) Deployment Guide
NIST SP 800-82 R2 Guide to Industrial Control Systems (ICS) Security
NIST SP 800-83 Guide to Malware Incident Prevention and Handling for Desktops and Laptops
NIST SP 800-84 Guide to Test, Training, and Exercise Programs for IT Plans and Capabilities
NIST SP 800-85A-4 PIV Card Application and Middleware Interface Test Guidelines
NIST SP 800-85B-4 PIV Data Model Test Guidelines - Draft
NIST SP 800-86 Guide to Integrating Forensic Techniques into Incident Response

NIST SP 1800-4a & 4b	Mobile Device Security: Cloud and Hybrid Builds
NIST SP 1800-4c	Mobile Device Security: Cloud and Hybrid Builds
NIST SP 1800-5	IT Asset Management: Financial Services
NIST SP 1800-6	Domain Name Systems-Based Electronic Mail Security
NIST SP 1800-7	Situational Awareness for Electric Utilities
NIST SP 1800-8	Securing Wireless Infusion Pumps
NIST SP 1800-9a & 9b	Access Rights Management for the Financial Services Sector
NIST SP 1800-9c	Access Rights Management for the Financial Services Sector - How To Guide
NIST SP 1800-11a & 11b	Data Integrity Recovering from Ransomware and Other Destructive Events
NIST SP 1800-11c	Data Integrity Recovering from Ransomware and Other Destructive Events - How To Guide
NIST SP 1800-12	Derived Personal Identity Verification (PIV) Credentials
NISTIR 7298 R2	Glossary of Key Information Security Terms
NISTIR 7316	Assessment of Access Control Systems
NISTIR 7497	Security Architecture Design Process for Health Information Exchanges (HIEs)
NISTIR 7511 R4 V1.2	Security Content Automation Protocol (SCAP) Version 1.2 Validation Program Test Requirements
NISTIR 7628 R1 Vol 1	Guidelines for Smart Grid Cybersecurity - Architecture, and High-Level Requirements
NISTIR 7628 R1 Vol 2	Guidelines for Smart Grid Cybersecurity - Privacy and the Smart Grid
NISTIR 7628 R1 Vol 3	Guidelines for Smart Grid Cybersecurity - Supportive Analyses and References
NISTIR 7756	CAESARS Framework Extension: An Enterprise Continuous Monitoring Technical Refer
NISTIR 7788	Security Risk Analysis of Enterprise Networks Using Probabilistic Attack Graphs
NISTIR 7823	Advanced Metering Infrastructure Smart Meter Upgradeability Test Framework
NISTIR 7874	Guidelines for Access Control System Evaluation Metrics
NISTIR 7904	Trusted Geolocation in the Cloud: Proof of Concept Implementation
NISTIR 7924	Reference Certificate Policy
NISTIR 7987	Policy Machine: Features, Architecture, and Specification
NISTIR 8006	NIST Cloud Computing Forensic Science Challenges
NISTIR 8011 Vol 1	Automation Support for Security Control Assessments
NISTIR 8011 Vol 2	Automation Support for Security Control Assessments
NISTIR 8040	Measuring the Usability and Security of Permuted Passwords on Mobile Platforms
NISTIR 8053	De-Identification of Personal Information
NISTIR 8054	NSTIC Pilots: Catalyzing the Identity Ecosystem
NISTIR 8055	Derived Personal Identity Verification (PIV) Credentials (DPC) Proof of Concept Research
NISTIR 8060	Guidelines for the Creation of Interoperable Software Identification (SWID) Tags
NISTIR 8062	Introduction to Privacy Engineering and Risk Management in Federal Systems
NISTIR 8074 Vol 1 & Vol 2	Strategic U.S. Government Engagement in International Standardization to Achieve U.S. Objectives for Cybersecurity
NISTIR 8080	Usability and Security Considerations for Public Safety Mobile Authentication
NISTIR 8089	An Industrial Control System Cybersecurity Performance Testbed
NISTIR 8112	Attribute Metadata - Draft
NISTIR 8135	Identifying and Categorizing Data Types for Public Safety Mobile Applications
NISTIR 8138	Vulnerability Description Ontology (VDO)
NISTIR 8144	Assessing Threats to Mobile Devices & Infrastructure
NISTIR 8151	Dramatically Reducing Software Vulnerabilities
NISTIR 8170	The Cybersecurity Framework
NISTIR 8176	Security Assurance Requirements for Linux Application Container Deployments
NISTIR 8179	Criticality Analysis Process Model
NISTIR 8183	Cybersecurity Framework Manufacturing Profile
NISTIR 8192	Enhancing Resilience of the Internet and Communications Ecosystem
Whitepaper	Cybersecurity Framework Manufacturing Profile
Whitepaper	NIST Framework for Improving Critical Infrastructure Cybersecurity
Whitepaper	Challenging Security Requirements for US Government Cloud Computing Adoption
FIPS PUBS 140-2	Security Requirements for Cryptographic Modules
FIPS PUBS 140-2 Annex A	Approved Security Functions
FIPS PUBS 140-2 Annex B	Approved Protection Profiles
FIPS PUBS 140-2 Annex C	Approved Random Number Generators
FIPS PUBS 140-2 Annex D	Approved Key Establishment Techniques
FIPS PUBS 180-4	Secure Hash Standard (SHS)
FIPS PUBS 186-4	Digital Signature Standard (DSS)
FIPS PUBS 197	Advanced Encryption Standard (AES)
FIPS PUBS 198-1	The Keyed-Hash Message Authentication Code (HMAC)
FIPS PUBS 199	Standards for Security Categorization of Federal Information and Information Systems
FIPS PUBS 200	Minimum Security Requirements for Federal Information and Information Systems
FIPS PUBS 201-2	Personal Identity Verification (PIV) of Federal Employees and Contractors
FIPS PUBS 202	SHA-3 Standard: Permutation-Based Hash and Extendable-Output Functions
DHS Study	DHS Study on Mobile Device Security
OMB A-130 / FISMA	OMB A-130/Federal Information Security Modernization Act
GAO	Federal Information System Controls Audit Manual

DoD	
UFC 3-430-11	Boiler Control Systems
UFC 4-010-06	Cybersecurity of Facility-Related Control Systems
FC 4-141-05N	Navy and Marine Corps Industrial Control Systems Monitoring Stations
MIL-HDBK-232A	RED/BLACK Engineering-Installation Guidelines
MIL-HDBK 1195	Radio Frequency Shielded Enclosures
TM 5-601	Supervisory Control and Data Acquisition (SCADA) Systems for C4ISR Facilities
ESTCP	Facility-Related Control Systems Cybersecurity Guideline
ESTCP	Facility-Related Control Systems Ver 4.0
DoD	Self-Assessing Security Vulnerabilities & Risks of Industrial Controls
DoD	Program Manager's Guidebook for Integrating the Cybersecurity Risk Management Framework (RMF) into the System Acquisition Lifecycle
DoD	Advanced Cyber Industrial Control System Tactics, Techniques, and Procedures (ACI TTP)
DoD 4140.1	Supply Chain Materiel Management Procedures
AFI 17-2NAS	Network Attack System (NAS) Vol. 1, 2 & 3
AFI 17-2ACD	Air Force Cyberspace Defense (ACD) Vol. 1, 2 & 3
AFI 10-1703	Air Force Cyberspace Training Publications
AFPD 17-2	Air Force Cyberspace Operations
AFI 17-2CSCS	Air Force Cyberspace Security and Control System (CSCS) Vol. 1, 2 & 3

www.ingramcontent.com/pod-product-compliance
Lightning Source LLC
LaVergne TN
LVHW082128070326
832902LV00040B/2984